**INTRODUCING
ISSUES WITH
OPPOSING
VIEWPOINTS®**

Cyberbullying

Lauri S. Friedman, *Book Editor*

GREENHAVEN PRESS
A part of Gale, Cengage Learning

GALE
CENGAGE Learning™

Detroit • New York • San Francisco • New Haven, Conn • Waterville, Maine • London

Christine Nasso, *Publisher*
Elizabeth Des Chenes, *Managing Editor*

For more information, contact:
Greenhaven Press
27500 Drake Rd.
Farmington Hills, MI 48331-3535
Or you can visit our Internet site at gale.cengage.com

For product information and technology assistance, contact us at

Gale Customer Support, 1-800-877-4253
For permission to use material from this text or product, submit all requests online at
www.cengage.com/permissions

Further permissions questions can be e-mailed to permissionrequest@cengage.com

Articles in Greenhaven Press anthologies are often edited for length to meet page requirements. In addition, original titles of these works are changed to clearly present the main thesis and to explicitly indicate the author's opinion. Every effort is made to ensure that Greenhaven Press accurately reflects the original intent of the authors. Every effort has been made to trace the owners of copyrighted material.

Cover image copyright © Ilja Masik, 2010. Used under license from Shutterstock.com.

LIBRARY OF CONGRESS CATALOGING-IN-PUBLICATION DATA

Cyberbullying / Lauri S. Friedman, book editor.
  p. cm. -- (Introducing issues with opposing viewpoints)
Includes bibliographical references and index.
ISBN 978-0-7377-5117-8 (hardcover)
1. Cyberbullying--Juvenile literature. 2. Computer crimes--Juvenile literature. 3. Cyberbullying--United States--Juvenile literature. 4. Computer crimes--United States --Juvenile literature. I. Freidman, Lauri S.
HV6773.2.C925 2010
302.3--dc22

2010034506

Printed in the United States of America
3 4 5 6 7 14 13 12 11

Contents

Foreword

Indulging in a wide spectrum of ideas, beliefs, and perspectives is a critical cornerstone of democracy. After all, it is often debates over differences of opinion, such as whether to legalize abortion, how to treat prisoners, or when to enact the death penalty, that shape our society and drive it forward. Such diversity of thought is frequently regarded as the hallmark of a healthy and civilized culture. As the Reverend Clifford Schutjer of the First Congregational Church in Mansfield, Ohio, declared in a 2001 sermon, "Surrounding oneself with only like-minded people, restricting what we listen to or read only to what we find agreeable is irresponsible. Refusing to entertain doubts once we make up our minds is a subtle but deadly form of arrogance." With this advice in mind, Introducing Issues with Opposing Viewpoints books aim to open readers' minds to the critically divergent views that comprise our world's most important debates.

Introducing Issues with Opposing Viewpoints simplifies for students the enormous and often overwhelming mass of material now available via print and electronic media. Collected in every volume is an array of opinions that captures the essence of a particular controversy or topic. Introducing Issues with Opposing Viewpoints books embody the spirit of nineteenth-century journalist Charles A. Dana's axiom: "Fight for your opinions, but do not believe that they contain the whole truth, or the only truth." Absorbing such contrasting opinions teaches students to analyze the strength of an argument and compare it to its opposition. From this process readers can inform and strengthen their own opinions, or be exposed to new information that will change their minds. Introducing Issues with Opposing Viewpoints is a mosaic of different voices. The authors are statesmen, pundits, academics, journalists, corporations, and ordinary people who have felt compelled to share their experiences and ideas in a public forum. Their words have been collected from newspapers, journals, books, speeches, interviews, and the Internet, the fastest growing body of opinionated material in the world.

Introducing Issues with Opposing Viewpoints shares many of the well-known features of its critically acclaimed parent series, Opposing Viewpoints. The articles are presented in a pro/con format, allowing readers to absorb divergent perspectives side by side. Active reading questions preface each viewpoint, requiring the student to approach the material thoughtfully and carefully. Useful charts, graphs, and cartoons supplement each article. A thorough introduction provides readers with crucial background on an issue. An annotated bibliography points the reader toward articles, books, and Web sites that contain additional information on the topic. An appendix of organizations to contact contains a wide variety of charities, nonprofit organizations, political groups, and private enterprises that each hold a position on the issue at hand. Finally, a comprehensive index allows readers to locate content quickly and efficiently.

Introducing Issues with Opposing Viewpoints is also significantly different from Opposing Viewpoints. As the series title implies, its presentation will help introduce students to the concept of opposing viewpoints, and learn to use this material to aid in critical writing and debate. The series' four-color, accessible format makes the books attractive and inviting to readers of all levels. In addition, each viewpoint has been carefully edited to maximize a reader's understanding of the content. Short but thorough viewpoints capture the essence of an argument. A substantial, thought-provoking essay question placed at the end of each viewpoint asks the student to further investigate the issues raised in the viewpoint, compare and contrast two authors' arguments, or consider how one might go about forming an opinion on the topic at hand. Each viewpoint contains sidebars that include at-a-glance information and handy statistics. A Facts About section located in the back of the book further supplies students with relevant facts and figures.

Following in the tradition of the Opposing Viewpoints series, Greenhaven Press continues to provide readers with invaluable exposure to the controversial issues that shape our world. As John Stuart Mill once wrote: "The only way in which a human being can make some approach to knowing the whole of a subject is by hearing what can be said about it by persons of every variety of opinion and studying all modes in which it can be looked at by every character of mind. No wise man ever acquired his wisdom in any mode but this." It is to this principle that Introducing Issues with Opposing Viewpoints books are dedicated.

Introduction

A
s cyberbullying becomes an increasingly common experience for teens around the world, educators, psychiatrists, and other experts wonder whether it is more dangerous or destructive than traditional bullying. On the one hand, it is argued that cyberbullying is not as devastating as traditional bullying because kids need not come face-to-face with their tormentor; in fact, a simple and swift shutting of the laptop can successfully separate victim from aggressor. On the other hand, it is argued that cyberbullying is a more serious problem than traditional bullying because of the way in which the Internet encourages anonymous cruelty and mob mentality and also reaches more people.

Cyberbullying is, by its nature, limited to verbal rather than physical insults, and this is one reason some say that cyberbullying is not as serious a problem as traditional, or playground, bullying. In traditional bullying, kids must suffer both the humiliation of being called names along with the pain of being kicked, slapped, punched, or worse. As columnist Helen A.S. Popkin has put it, "I, personally, would rather be bullied online, because it's super-duper hard for anyone to IM you a purple nurple."[1] Or, put another way, "A bus stop beat down is recognizably and immediately more damaging than an acronym-rich text threat."[2]

Polls have confirmed that teens themselves do not seem to feel particularly threatened by cyberbullying. A 2007 survey by the National Crime Prevention Council and Harris Interactive, for example, confirmed that cyberbullying is common—about 43 percent of students polled said they had experienced some form of it within the past year. However, the overwhelming majority—61 percent of boys and 52 percent of girls—reported that they were "not bothered" by it. So although cyberbullying is a common occurrence, it is not one that many teens view as particularly critical or threatening. "Just as it can be meaner than bullying in person, it can also be easier to block or ignore," says tech blogger Anastasia Goodstein. "Teens view this issue as something that can be controlled by either just not responding, blocking the bully or through moderators intervening online. To them, it's not an issue schools should be addressing."[3] Goodstein personally polled teenagers about whether they had ever been a victim of cyberbullying and received answers such as "This girl was mad because I was talking to a boy she liked. I just ignored it," and, "A boy continued to call me a b***h and I just blocked him and I was never bothered again."[4] Because they can control the extent to which the bully has access to them, these and other teens view cyberbullying as less of a threat than traditional bullying.

Yet others view cyberbullying as a greater threat than traditional bullying because of the very public, and fiercely bandwagon, nature of the Internet. Because people say things online that they would not necessarily say in real life, cyberbullying can cut deeper and be more vicious than in-person bullying. In addition, traditional bullying tends to be witnessed by just a handful of people and is over when bully and victim part ways; bullying on the Internet, however, can be witnessed by thousands of people and exists until content is removed from cyberspace, which can be very difficult. For example, it took nearly a month to remove a Facebook page that was created to torment one Swedish girl ("Those of us who hate Stina Johansson" was the name of the page). Finally, on the playground, there are typically only a handful of bullies in any given class; the Internet, however, allows every teen with an Internet connection and something nasty to say to gang up on peers. Indeed, the Internet tends to foster a cruel and unrelenting mob-mentality situation in which people gang up on others until dozens, even hundreds, of people are participating in an assault.

Indeed, the public and 24-7 nature of the Internet makes cyberbullying a threat from which teens often feel they have no escape. "At least with conventional bullying the victim is left alone on evenings and weekends," says Ann Frisén, professor of psychology at the University of Gothenburg. "Victims of internet bullying, or cyberbullying, have no refuge. Victims may be harassed continuously via SMS [short message service text messaging] and websites, and the information spreads very quickly and may be difficult to remove."[5] Frisén studies the effect of different types of bullying on teens and has found that although technology can be shut off, the fact that the bullying continues to exist in cyberspace has a psychologically devastating effect on many teens. "The kids who beat you up in school didn't used to follow you home," says cyberbullying expert Parry Aftab. "Now they do."[6]

That cyberbullying is more serious than traditional bullying is evidenced by the number of teenagers who have committed suicide after enduring it. Megan Meier, Jessica Logan, and Ryan Patrick Halligan are just a few of the teens who have killed themselves after suffering a relentless bullying campaign from their peers. Fifteen-year-old Phoebe Prince, for example, hanged herself in March 2010 after experiencing more than three months of taunts, threats, and abuse. So did fifteen-year-old Gail Jones, a British girl who took her life in 2000 after receiving dozens of silent calls on her cell phone every half hour. Teens who are bullied on the playground may show bruises and scars, but very rarely does the bullying result in death.

Whether cyberbullying is worse than traditional bullying is perhaps less important than what can be done to prevent both from occurring. To this end, the viewpoints in *Introducing Issues with Opposing Viewpoints: Cyberbullying* explore ways to prevent cyberbullying, whether cyberbullying should be criminalized, and how serious the problem is. Noted experts and informed observers offer compelling perspectives on the subject, while reading comprehension questions and thought-provoking essay prompts encourage students to form their own opinions on the matter.

Notes
1. Helen A.S. Popkin, "Cyberbullying Laws Won't Save Your Children," MSNBC, May 15, 2009. http://today.msnbc.msn.com/id/30751310/ns/technology_and_science_tech_and_gadgets/.
2. Helen A.S. Popkin, "Cyberbullying Really Is That Bad," MSNBC, July 5, 2007. http://today.msnbc.msn.com/id/19620683/ns/technology_and_science_tech_and_gadgets/.
3. Anastasia Goodstein, "Most Teens 'Not Bothered' by Cyberbullying," *Totally Wired*, May 2, 2007. http://totallywired.ypulse.com/archives/2007/05/most_teens_not_bothered_by_cyb_1.php.
4. Quoted in Goodstein, "Most Teens 'Not Bothered' by Cyberbullying."
5. Quoted in University of Gothenburg, "Cyberbullying: A Growing Problem," *Science Daily*, February 22, 2010. www.sciencedaily.com/releases/2010/02/100222104939.htm.
6. Quoted in Rob Rogers, "Cyberbullying Expert to Lead Panel," *Billings (MT) Gazette*, June 15, 2010. http://billingsgazette.com/news/local/education/article_cdc70a8c-790b-11df-bf35-001cc4c 002e0.html.

Chapter 1

Is Cyberbullying a Serious Problem?

Cyberbullying has become a common experience for teens around the world. It has the potential to become a more serious problem than traditional bullying.

Cyberbullying Is a Serious Problem

Susan Hayes

"Increasing reports of youth suicide, as well as school violence, in the United States appear to be related to cyber-bullying."

In the following viewpoint, Susan Hayes argues that cyberbullying has become a serious problem. She explains that the impact of cyberbullying can be devastating, resulting in suicides or even school murders. The incidents result from using the Internet, or even cell phones, to post information meant to hurt a person or damage his or her reputation. Hayes points out that cyberbullies are typically former close friends of the victims and are not just "anonymous thugs in cyberspace." When the abuse gets increasingly worse, Hayes contends that one of the best solutions is having friends who speak up against the bullying.

Susan Hayes is a contributor to *Current Health 2,* a *Weekly Reader* publication that supports the development of writing skills, reading comprehension, and vocabulary for all learners.

AS YOU READ, CONSIDER THE FOLLOWING QUESTIONS:
1. According to the author, what percentage range of teens receive abuse and threats through the Internet?
2. Who does Hayes claim are the typical cyberbullies?
3. According to WiredSafety.org, as cited by the author, what three things should a victim of cyberbullying do?

Outgoing, smart, pretty, and a three-sport varsity athlete, Mary Ellen, now 19, from New Jersey, is not the kind of teen you would expect to be bullied. Yet for months during her freshman year at a private, all-girls' high school, every time she turned on her computer, a barrage of IMs and attacks on MySpace calling her slut and whore awaited her.

That wasn't the worst of it. Someone else, pretending to be her, used her password to create messages that said mean things about her classmates. Then there was the manipulated picture of Mary Ellen, complete with the addition of horns and the label "Loser," posted on a photo-sharing Web site for all the world to see.

Torment on the Web

Online harassment has a name: cyberbullying. That means "using the Internet or cell phones to send hurtful messages or post information that's designed to damage the reputation or friendships of others," according to Nancy Willard, executive director of the Center for Safe and Responsible Internet Use (CSRIU) and the author of *Cyberbullying and Cyberthreats*. No one knows the exact number of teens who are on the receiving end, but it's significant. "Survey data ranges from 7 percent to 55 percent," says Willard. "My guess is it's somewhere in between."

The impact can be devastating. Increasing reports of youth suicide, as well as school violence, in the United States appear to be related to cyberbullying. Suicides have occurred in South Korea, too, and a school murder in Japan might have been related to cyberbullying. Although many experts say adults have been slow to respond to the problem, that may be changing. School administrators and politicians are trying to crack down on cyberbullying once it starts and to prevent it from happening. Until they do, here's what you need to know.

Best Friends Forever? Not Always

First, it helps to understand who cyberbullies typically are. Anonymous thugs in cyberspace? Not usually: Most targets know their aggressors, often quite well. "Almost 50 percent of cyberbullying incidents involve former close friends," says Parry Aftab, a lawyer and the executive director of WiredSafety.org, an online safety and help group. In Mary Ellen's case, it was her former best friend.

Why does someone go from best friend to bully? Often out of anger, revenge, jealousy, or frustration, says Aftab. Mary Ellen's former best friend accused her of "stealing her boyfriend," even after initially assuring Mary Ellen that the guy was only a friend and that she had no problem with the two dating.

As frequently happens with cyberbullying, Mary Ellen's former friend also recruited an army of accomplices. "To convince them that I was a horrible person, she copied and pasted my screen name onto

Teens today are so wired into computers and cell phones that asking them to not use them is not a practical solution to the problem of cyberbullying.

messages that she wrote saying bad things about them and then said to them, 'Look what Mary Ellen's saying about you,'" Mary Ellen recalls. Indeed, one of the main rationales that cyberbullies give for their actions is that their target "has done something mean themselves and therefore deserves it," says Willard.

Even if you and your best friend never fight, you can still become a target. Although more girls than boys are likely to experience cyberbullying, about a third of all teens who use the Internet say they have received a threatening message, had their private e-mails or text messages forwarded without their consent, or had an embarrassing picture or rumor about them posted online, according to a Pew Internet & American Life Project 2006 survey. Most teens who experience cyberbullying report feeling embarrassed, frustrated, angry, sad, helpless, and/or scared, says Justin Patchin, a leading cyberbullying researcher and assistant professor of criminal justice at the University of Wisconsin–Eau Claire.

Mary Ellen can relate to that. "I was crying every night, I couldn't eat, and I had stress-induced stomachaches," she says. "Also, at my school we used computers in class and for doing homework. Because it got to the point where I didn't even want to turn mine on, my grades went down from A's to C's. I wanted to leave the school."

> **FAST FACT**
>
> A 2008 study by researchers at the Yale University School of Medicine found a connection between bullying, being bullied, and an increased risk for teen suicide.

What's a Teen to Do?

Mary Ellen didn't leave, but she did instinctively do the three things that now, as a WiredSafety.org Teenangel (a specially trained volunteer who visits schools to spread the word about Internet safety), she tells others to do: Stop, block, and tell. "I never once wrote back," she says, "because I knew they wanted a reaction. I also blocked the screen name of whoever sent the message. Finally, I told my mom. That was the hardest part. I wanted to handle it on my own."

Most teens who are cyberbullied feel the same way. "I have a list of 56 different reasons kids have given me for why they don't tell their

A Growing Problem

More than one-third of Internet-using adolescents report that they have experienced cyberbullying, some so much that they feared for their safety.

Types of Victimization

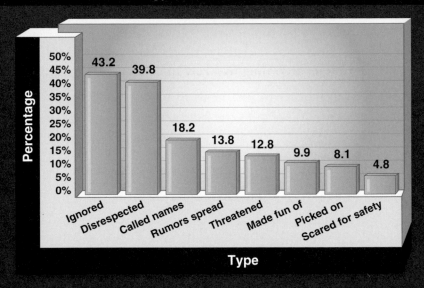

Victimization by Location

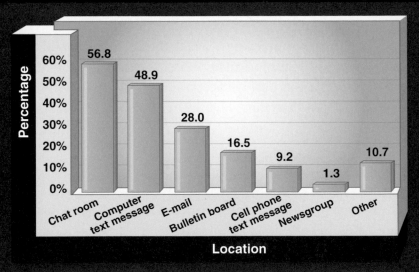

parents," says Aftab. One of the most common is the fear that parents will take away a cell phone or computer privileges. Experts say cutting off online access is rarely the solution. "Being connected is everything to this generation," says Patchin. "Telling a kid who is being cyberbullied to just stay off the Internet is like telling a kid who is being bullied at school to just not go to school."

Although the majority of cyberbullying incidents take place outside school, they often spill over, as in Mary Ellen's case. She was blackballed from her regular lunch table, stared down and insulted as she walked through the halls, and laughed at when she got an answer wrong in class. A growing number of school districts believe that this spillover effect gives them justification to punish cyberbullies, even though schools typically have little legal authority over students' speech or conduct off campus. Some states are even considering new laws that would allow schools to intervene.

Even so, experts say, many school administrators are uncertain how far their reach extends and how to make a cyberbully stop. After the dean at Mary Ellen's school found out what was going on, she pulled Mary Ellen and her tormentor out of the cafeteria one day and told them to say they were sorry. "I wasn't sure what I was saying sorry for," Mary Ellen says, "but I said it anyway." In any case, it didn't help. The abuse continued.

It turns out the people with the clout to finally stop it were not adults but older students who were Mary Ellen's varsity soccer teammates. They didn't appreciate it when the tormentor and her minions, members of the junior varsity team, started bullying Mary Ellen during practice. "It was positive peer pressure," says Mary Ellen. "They basically said, 'Cut the crap.' Then other kids started sticking up for me too." That doesn't surprise Willard, who says, "One of the best protections against cyberbullying is having friends who speak up and say that's not OK."

Although the effects still linger, Mary Ellen, who ended up thriving at the high school she once wished she could leave, wants teens who are being cyberbullied to know that life—and life online—can be sweet again. Now a college freshman, Mary Ellen says, "My two best friends are from my high school. We're at different colleges, but we all have [computers], and we video chat every night."

Fighting Cyberbullying with TV

To help put a stop to cyberbullying, Sony Creative Software, the Ad Council, and the National Crime Prevention Council are banking on "old" technology—specifically, that ancient relic called television. Last fall [2007], they teamed up to run a contest, inviting both professional video producers and schools to submit public service announcements (PSAs) that raise awareness about cyberbullying. The winning entries—one created by a pro and one by a school group—[aired] on national TV.

Justin Patchin, an expert on cyberbullying, helped judge the contest, along with Barry Sonnenfeld, the director of *Men in Black* and *The Addams Family*, and Steve Oedekerk, the writer of *Evan Almighty* and the producer, director, and writer of *Barnyard*. Patchin says he hopes the PSAs will help adults better understand cyberbullying and recognize its seriousness. "And hopefully, the cyberbullies themselves will see them and realize the harm they're causing," he says.

EVALUATING THE AUTHOR'S ARGUMENTS:

Hayes quotes and mentions several sources to support the points she makes in her essay. Make a list of everyone she uses to support her argument, including their credentials and the nature of their comments. Then analyze her sources. Are they credible? Are they well qualified to speak on this subject? Why or why not?

The Seriousness of the Cyberbullying Problem Is Exaggerated

Arizona Daily Wildcat

"*Pretending that there is no difference between criticism— even mean criticism— and threats is both stupid and dangerous.*"

The following viewpoint was an editorial written by a student at the University of Arizona. In it, the student argues that society overreacts to cyberbullying; cyberbullying is nothing more than people making their opinions and criticisms public in an online forum. Even though some of these people choose to express themselves in a mean or hurtful manner, the author argues, their opinions are protected by the First Amendment. The author contends that Americans have no obligation to be nice to each other—their right to free speech allows them to say nasty things about one another in person, and this right should remain intact when they say such things on the Internet. The author rejects the basis of cyberbullying harassment cases, maintaining that people need to be thicker skinned if someone writes something mean about them online. The author concludes that telling America's students to stifle their opinions teaches them the wrong message about free speech and violates their First Amendment rights.

The *Arizona Daily Wildcat* is the student newspaper of the University of Arizona.

AS YOU READ, CONSIDER THE FOLLOWING QUESTIONS:
1. Who masks their intentions under the guise of promoting "safety" and preventing "harassment," according to the author?
2. Who is Katherine Evans and how does she factor into the author's argument?
3. What happened on February 2, 2009, and how does this event lend support to the author's argument?

T he First Amendment doesn't have any fine print. There aren't any puling [whiny] little equivocations, any "buts" or "excepts." The amendment protects freedom of speech, period.

This is why the First Amendment presents an ever-present threat to those who would seek to stifle us in the name of hurt feelings. And that is why we must be ever on alert to spot attempts to keep us from expressing "hurtful" thoughts. They don't trumpet their intention of censorship; they mask their intentions in the guise of promoting "safety" and preventing "harassment," even if those elements are in no way relevant.

A Wrongful Suspension

The *New York Times* reported Saturday [July 25, 2009] that Katherine Evans, a former high school senior and honor student at a Miami high school, was suing her former principal for ordering her suspension. Evans had been suspended for posting an angry rant against an English teacher of hers on Facebook. "Sarah Phelps is the worst teacher I've ever met!" she wrote.

After a few days, Evans took the post down. Two months later, she was suspended for "cyberbullying harassment." She's suing in order

A teenager trades insults online with another user. Cyberbullying is considered a form of free speech and is protected under the First Amendment to the U.S. Constitution.

to remove the suspension from her record because she feels, quite rightly, that she was unfairly charged.

Free Speech Protects Mean Speech

Had Evans threatened her teacher, the school would have had a case. But she didn't. Pretending that there is no difference between criticism—even mean criticism—and threats is both stupid and dangerous. For one thing, it threatens to quash legitimate criticism; for another, it corrodes the seriousness of genuine threats.

What's particularly disturbing is that Evans is being punished for making her views public. As Howard Simon, executive director of the American Civil Liberties Union, told the *Times*, "If Katie Evans said what she said over burgers with her friends at the mall, there is no question it would be protected by free speech." Posting something on the Internet does not render the First Amendment null and void.

The very notion of "cyberbullying" is preposterous when applied to an adult—particularly a teacher. If a teacher is prepared to crumple up and sob at the thought that one of her students might not like her, she'd better start looking for another job.

Wrong to Stifle Students' Opinions

What sort of lesson does this teach America's students? One of Evans's fellow classmates told the British newspaper, the *Guardian*: "She made her dislike for her far too public. She messed up." Is that what we want students to learn—that you shouldn't make your "dislike" of anyone public? That expressing a negative opinion of an authority figure is something to be punished?

As college students, it's easy to feel distant from this sort of thing. Sure, they can get away with treating students like that in the public schools, but that could never happen here, right?

Think again.

Most Teens Have Not Been Cyberbullied

The majority of teenagers have not been victims of cyberbullying which has led some people to claim the problem has been overstated.

Have you, personally, ever experienced any of the following things online?	Yes	No
Someone taking a private e-mail, IM (instant message), or text message you sent them and forwarding it to someone else or posting it where others could see it	15%	85%
Someone spreading a rumor about you online	13%	87%
Someone sending you a threatening or aggressive e-mail, IM, or text message	13%	87%
Someone posting an embarrassing picture of you online without your permission	6%	94%
Answered "yes" to any of the four previous questions	32%	68%

Taken from: Amanda Lenhart, "Data Memo: Cyberbullying and Online Teens," Pew Internet & American Life Project, June 27, 2007 and "Parents and Teens Survey," October–November 2006.

You Cannot Force People to Be Nice

As the *Daily Wildcat* reported in [a recent column called] Police Beat, a student was referred to the Dean of Students Office Feb. 2 [2009] for sending "unwanted" e-mails to a former professor who he felt had been biased against him.

Instead of telling him to get lost, the professor decided to report these e-mails—which, judging from the excerpts published, were neither threatening nor even particularly mean—to the police. Now, apparently, expressing any criticism of a professor whatsoever will earn you a visit to the Dean of Students Office.

We'd all like the world to be a nice place. We'd all prefer that people express their feelings in a pleasant way. But the world doesn't work like that, and attempting to enforce "niceness" by referring its violators to the principal's office, or the police, isn't merely unconstitutional. It's also doomed to failure.

EVALUATING THE AUTHOR'S ARGUMENTS:

The author of this viewpoint contends that all speech—even mean, nasty, or hateful speech—deserves protection under the First Amendment. What do you think? Do you agree that there should be no limits on free speech, or are there some kinds of speech that you think do not deserve constitutional protection? Come up with two or three examples of controversial speech and state whether or not you think it deserves constitutional protection, and why.

Cyberbullying Is Worse than Traditional Bullying

Shanna Hogan

"[Cyberbul-lying] can be a lot worse than normal bullying."

Cyberbullying is more damaging than traditional schoolyard bullying, argues Shanna Hogan in the following viewpoint. She discusses how online bullying has grown as more kids use the Internet to anonymously attack and torment each other. Hogan contends that unlike traditional schoolyard bullying, there is little escape from cyberbullying —the mean comments or cruelly edited photos exist online twenty-four hours a day. Also, unlike schoolyard bullying, which is typically witnessed by only a handful of people, hundreds or thousands of people can witness cyberbullying, making the victim feel publicly humiliated to an extreme. Finally, the anonymity of the Internet encourages people to be more cruel and aggressive than they would be in real life, Hogan maintains. As a result, kids who are cyberbullied struggle with depression, self-esteem issues, anxiety, higher rates of school absence, and

Shanna Hogan, "Cyber Bully: The Schoolyard Bully Now Has a Screen Name," *Times Publications*, October 2008. Reproduced by permission of the publisher and the author.

suicide, she argues. For all these reasons Hogan concludes that cyber-bullying is more dangerous than traditional schoolyard bullying.

Hogan is an award-winning Arizona journalist and true crime author.

AS YOU READ, CONSIDER THE FOLLOWING QUESTIONS:
1. What percentage of kids say they were cyberbullied within the past year, as reported by Hogan?
2. According to the author, what did a report by the Crimes Against Children Research Center find about the number of teens who experience online harassment?
3. How many bullies will have a criminal record by the time they turn thirty, according to research from the U.S. Department of Education as reported by Hogan?

Thirteen-year-old Ryan Patrick Halligan turns on his bedroom computer and logs online for the last time.

For the past several months the Internet has become a virtual schoolyard for Ryan, where he has been bullied, threatened, harassed and humiliated through instant messages and e-mails.

The bullies called him a loser since he had a learning disability; because of his sweet, gentle demeanor, they spread rumors that he was gay.

The torment that once only took place at school is now relentless. But Ryan has a plan to put an end to the bullying. For good.

A Final Act of Desperation
And this last desperate act wasn't his first attempt to stop the humiliation.

To combat the "gay" rumor, the lanky teen spent all summer e-mailing and chatting online with one of the popular girls at school. By the time eighth grade started, he was convinced she was his "new girlfriend."

But when Ryan approached her he found their relationship to be a farce.

"You're just a loser," she told him, surrounded by all her friends. "I don't want anything to do with you. I was just joking."

In fact, she had posted their personal correspondence with Ryan online for the amusement of her friends.

For Ryan, a notably sensitive kid with a kind, tenderhearted personality, the experience was devastating. He never told his family what had happened; instead he went back online.

And this October night, in an online chat room, Ryan tells the bullies about his new plan.

"Tonight's the night," he writes, "you are going to read about in the paper tomorrow."

"It's about time," one of the bullies types back.

After his family is asleep, Ryan goes into the bathroom, strings up a noose and hangs himself.

Cyberbullying Is Different

Ryan was the victim of what has come to be known as cyber bullying—the use of the Internet, cell phones and other digital technology to harass, intimidate, threaten, mock and degrade an individual, sometimes with devastating consequences.

Experts say cyber bullying is a growing epidemic among young people. In fact, about 43 percent of teens say they have been the victim of cyber bullying within the past year, according to a report by the National Crime Prevention Council.

And as bullying has moved out of the schoolyard and onto the Web, experts say it has become more aggressive and invasive, leading to serious repercussions for kids who are often already struggling with a host of other adolescent issues. According to experts, its effects are leading to depression, low self esteem and problems at school, and in severe cases, like Ryan's, the torment can eventually turn tragic.

"I believe my son would have survived these incidents of bullying and humiliation if they took place before computers and the Internet," says Ryan's father, John Halligan. "It's one thing to be bullied and humiliated in front of a few kids . . . but it has to be a totally different experience than a generation ago, when these hurts and humiliation are now witnessed by a far larger, online adolescent audience."

Online Harassment Is Growing

The number of teens who experienced online harassment increased by 50 percent from 2000 to 2005, according to a report by the Crimes Against Children Research Center. The U.S. Centers for Disease Control and Prevention now consider cyber bullying an emerging adolescent health concern.

"It's proliferated particularly among young people as they spend more time online and become more computer savvy," says Dr. Sheri Bauman, an associate professor in the Department of Educational Psychology at the University of Arizona. "It seems to be increasing exponentially."

While this kind of bullying has occurred in different forms for as long as the Internet has existed, experts say it has really jumped in the past five years with the creation of social networking sites such as MySpace and Facebook.

Any technological tool can be used in cyber bullying, including e-mail, instant messaging and cell-phone text messages, says Robert Strom, a professor at Arizona State University's Division of Psychology in Education.

"For instance, in some high schools you might go to the online voting booth and select from the five people who you consider to be the fattest in the school," he says. "It's a way of humiliating people and making them feel helpless."

> ## FAST FACT
>
> According to a 2009 report published by the Anti-Defamation League, 35 percent of thirteen- to seventeen-year-olds reported having experienced at least one of the following forms of Internet harassment in the previous year: rude or nasty comments, rumors, and threatening or aggressive messages. Eight percent reported having been targeted monthly or more often.

The Changing Face of the Bully

Well-publicized cases include an incident at a Pittsburgh high school where 25 female students were harassed after an anonymous e-mail list went out ranking them sexually, including their names and photos. In Florida, a group of teens beat up another student in retaliation for on-line "trash talking" by the victim. But perhaps the most famous cyber bullying case involved 13-year-old Megan Meier, a [Missouri] girl who committed suicide after being tricked by the mother of a former friend, who had pretended to be a teenage boy who liked her on MySpace.

Experts say this type of humiliation is more damaging than traditional face-to-face bullying because it is more invasive, takes place in front of a much larger audience, occurs 24-7 and is permanently preserved.

"I think cyber bullying can change the face of a bully because you no longer have to have physical strength or intimidation, you just have to be a little computer savvy," says Rebecca Lahann, a director at the Phoenix-based non-profit group Not My Kid, which deals with adolescent issues, including cyber bullying. "It's not your stereotypical tough guy anymore; it could be the quiet, shy girl in the class."

Worse than Normal Bullying

Julianne Flory, 19, was used to being teased and shoved around at school. But when the bullying started happening in her bedroom on the Internet, she says it became truly frightening.

Common Types of Cyberbullying

Type	Definition
Flaming	A heated, online exchange
Harassment	Electronic messages that cause emotional distress
Denigration	Online postings of negative or false information about someone
Impersonation	Communicating negative, false information to others while impersonating someone
Outing and trickery	Electronically sharing or forwarding personal, secret information
Exclusion and ostracism	Removing or blocking people from buddy lists
Cyberstalking	Using technology to stalk and threaten a target
Happy slapping	Videotaping and electronically disseminating an instance of slapping someone

Taken from: Robin M. Kowalski, "Cyber Bullying," *Psychiatric Times*, vol. 25, no. 11, October 1, 2008.

Online bullying has grown as more kids use the Internet to personally attack each other.

"It can be a lot worse than normal bullying," she says. "The bully can put up messages where everyone can see them."

The group of teenage girls, who had conducted a bullying campaign against Flory since she was 13, found her online through a social networking Web site. At first, to obtain personal information, they pretended to be her friend, but she soon began receiving nasty, insulting messages, saying things like, "You look like an ugly slut," "you have no friends," and "we're going to get you tomorrow."

Flory tried to seek help through her teachers and the principal, but those efforts did not stop the messages.

"My school was so awful dealing with it," she says. "It was a joke."

Then the cruel abuse turned alarming.

"They threatened my family," she says. "And then they started to threaten to stab me."

After the death threats, Julianne printed out the messages and showed them to her father. The family took the messages to authorities and obtained harassment orders against the girls.

Today, as an adult, the pretty, curly-haired brunette is no longer a target of bullying. She teaches Judo, plans to study sports science in college and eventually wants to become a physical-education teacher. Still, the abuse she endured for years has left its mark.

"I became very depressed and still have low self belief and confidence," she says. "But I have great friends and family and have a good life, so overall they haven't beaten me."

Long-Term Effects

Cyber bullying can have devastating long-term effects for both the victims and the bullies, experts say.

One in four children who act as bullies in school will have a criminal record by the time they reach the age of 30, according to research from the U.S. Department of Education. As adults, research shows bullies are also more likely to have unstable relationships.

"Years ago it was thought that bullies were kids with low self esteem," says Sam Cianfarano, a former elementary-school principal in the Paradise Valley [Arizona] School District and a director at Not My Kid. "Research indicates that actually these are kids with high self esteem. They just like to have control and power and to exert that power over other people."

"Greater Potential for Damage"

Scott Smith may look like a tough guy. But his military haircut and large frame run contrary to his soft-spoken, sweet demeanor.

Years ago, however, Smith was a bully.

"Whatever I could do to threaten, harass, intimidate, scare—those were my favorite tools," says Smith, a Phoenix resident. "I'd rather be feared than respected. That was my mentality."

After years of picking on other students, one day Smith says he saw another bully tormenting a kid and decided that wasn't who he wanted to be.

"I started to see how my bullying was affecting others," he says. "By being a bully, I didn't have any friends. I would try and push people away."

Today, Smith, now 29, works with Not My Kid, speaking at schools about his past, hoping to be an example for kids and to discourage bullying.

"The Internet, the chat rooms, the cell phones are really just a whole other world of how you can threaten, intimidate and harass," he says. "I can see a greater potential for damage for students."

About 35 percent of kids say they have been threatened online, according to a study by iSafe, an organization dedicated to Internet-safety education. Nearly one in five have had it happen more than once.

Victims of cyber bullying are more likely to suffer from anxiety, depression, lower self esteem and higher rates of school absence.

Kids involved in the more severe instances of online harassment also tend to have more psychosocial problems—exhibiting aggression, getting in trouble at school and having poor relationships with their parents. . . .

Protecting Kids from Cyberbullies

After Ryan Halligan committed suicide on October 6, 2003, his father went online to try to piece together what had happened. Halligan discovered that Ryan had unintentionally installed a program that archived the Internet conversations he had had with the bullies.

"That really unraveled the mystery, because I started to find the conversations not only with the kids who had bullied him for being potentially gay, but also between him and the girl," Halligan says.

He also discovered Ryan had conducted Internet searches for ways to "painlessly kill" himself.

After confronting the bullies, Halligan set off on a crusade, touring schools across the country, to make children and parents more aware of the dangers of suicide and cyber bullying.

"I think as parents we let kids use technology at too young of an age," he says. "I think we would have avoided a lot of this hurt had we had put restrictions on his Internet use and monitored what he was doing online."

Halligan also successfully lobbied for new anti-bullying and suicide-prevention rules for schools.

By telling his son's story, he hopes to change the minds of people about Internet harassment and just how damaging it can truly be.

"Ryan was just a sweet kid, kind, gentle and sensitive," he says. "He wasn't a fighter. We need to celebrate those kids and not make them feel like they're inadequate."

EVALUATING THE AUTHORS' ARGUMENTS:

Hogan explains that cyberbullying is particularly damaging because, unlike schoolyard bullying, which takes place before or after school, there is no escape from cyberbullying—it exists around the clock on all of a person's electronic devices. But Helen A.S. Popkin, author of the following viewpoint, suggests that cyberbullying is not as bad as traditional bullying because one can physically separate oneself from the bully and turn off one's electronic gadgets. What do you think—is it easier or more difficult to escape from an online bully or a schoolyard bully? Why?

Cyberbullying Is Not Worse than Traditional Bullying

Helen A.S. Popkin

"I, personally, would rather be bullied online, because it's super-duper hard for anyone to IM you a purple nurple."

In the following viewpoint Helen A.S. Popkin argues that being bullied online is better than being bullied in person. She says that throughout history mean jerks have bullied weaker, more vulnerable people. Popkin is not surprised that people have used the format of the Internet to carry on this time-honored tradition, but she argues that online bullying is easier to escape than in-person bullying, and is thus easier to endure. Because online bullying is not that bad, Popkin argues, laws against it are an overreaction. She points out that the government cannot make it illegal to be mean, which in her opinion is all cyberbullying really is. She concludes that as long as online meanness does not become physical, there is nothing the government can or should do to prevent it.

Popkin writes about technology and social issues for MSNBC.

I s it better or worse to bully someone if you're using the Internet?

Worse apparently, according to lawmakers on the most recent "Won't somebody please think of the children?!" crusade in vogue. I, personally, would rather be bullied online, because it's super-duper hard for anyone to IM you a purple nurple [bruise].

The Wrong Response

Being harassed by anonymous jerks online, however, does not call for its own legislation. The latest attempt to outlaw in the intrinsic ugliness of the Internet, with all its "sexting" and "cyberbullying," is the recently reintroduced H.R. 1966 Act [a proposed U.S. House of Representatives bill], which proposes felony charges in language so vague, free speech advocates are positively apoplectic.

Amorphous language that endangers our free speech is probably just the thing that will continue to hang up H.R. 1966. But the fuss about a special law for the Inter-Webs sheds light on the broader issue that the lawmakers are confusing their principles with the medium. Outlawing cyberbullying is like outlawing bullying in a Southern accent. No one's pro bullies in any dialect, but you can't help wonder if someone's missing the point.

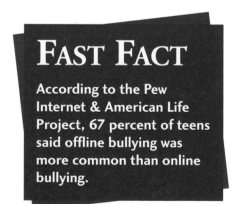

FAST FACT

According to the Pew Internet & American Life Project, 67 percent of teens said offline bullying was more common than online bullying.

Unlike traditional bullying, online bullying does not happen in person.

You know how shutting down the "erotic services" section on Craigslist won't stop sex workers, or eliminate their higher probability of becoming crime victims by the marginalized nature of the trade? Similarly, outlawing meanness on the Internet won't prevent hectors from preying on the weak on the Internet or turn jerks into saints in any aspect of their lives.

Not the Main Cause of Teen Suicide

Attention-grabbing headlines, spotlight-hungry politicians and Internet safety crusaders would have us believe that technology is killing our children by the school bus–load. H.R. 1966 is also known as the "Megan Meier Cyberbullying Prevention Act," named for the 13-year-old girl who suicided after she suffered extended harassment on MySpace.

The people behind another proposed law, the "School And Family Education about the Internet (SAFE Internet) Act," recruited as spokesperson the mother of a teenage girl who suffered public humiliation after her nude picture was "sexted" to hundreds of people. That girl also killed herself.

Many of the news stories about these tragic events flagrantly disregard the World Health Organization's media guidelines for reporting suicide thoroughly and without drama, so as not to incite media contagion—the proven event in which news coverage inspires copycat suicides, especially among teenagers.

Many of the stories either failed to mention, or otherwise buried the facts that Megan Meier had suicidal ideations before her MySpace ordeal or that the "sexting" victim had just attended the funeral of a friend who had recently killed herself, which increases suicide risk significantly.

When such stories are covered or laws are proposed, there is often little or no mention that the teenage suicide rate in the United States is wretchedly high, and was even before the pervasiveness of technology.

Government Cannot Legislate Parenting

Unfortunately, sensation rallies a mob more efficiently than adequate research and dissemination of critical information: how to recognize dangerous behavior, mental illness and suicide risk in teenagers, no matter the stressor. Case in point: In a recent *Huffington Post* blog entry, Rep. Linda Sanchez, D-Calif., defends H.R. 1966 in part by exploiting the ghosts of [the 1999 school shooting at] Columbine—inaccurately.

"According to a study by the United States Secret Service, being bullied is a risk factor for perpetrators of school violence, such as the kind that was unleashed with tragic results at Columbine High School in Colorado," Sanchez wrote.

In fact, the final report from the Secret Service and U.S. Department of Education found that there is no profile for school shooters. "Columbine" author Dave Cullen, whose decade-long coverage exploded this and other myths about the massacre, writes of the shooters, "They were not captains of the football team, but they were far more accepted than many of their schoolmates."

Still, if our government representatives insist we continue to consider preposterous proposed laws while keeping our faces straight, how about a law that mandates parents to actively engage in the lives of their children? Too much? Maybe then the government can outlaw gravity next so my poor babies don't have to worry about falling down and skinning their knees.

People Have a Right to Be Mean
Meanwhile, there are lots of ways I can get all the anonymity and nastiness of the Internet out of other media. There's calling you from a payphone, slipping nasty notes under your door, pinning a cat to your car, whatever.

Settle down. I won't do that (because it's crazy illegal already). But please, stop trying to legislate against meanness. People have a right to be mean. We need to draw the line somewhere, so meanness doesn't become beatings and such, but even the most brain-atrophied among us should be able to identify that distinction. And if not, well, it turns out we already have a whole mess of laws covering assault, battery, slander and libel.

It's not like Al Gore, [the former vice president who claims to have invented the Internet] invented psychos, too. And as long as there are bold souls out there creating shiny new media we can use for communication, some maladjusted jackass is going to go ahead and be, well, a maladjusted jackass with whatever they dream up. Laws, as much as possible, should leave the question of the medium aside and focus on the spirit of the issue. If they don't, lawmakers will forever be playing catch-up.

EVALUATING THE AUTHOR'S ARGUMENTS:

In this viewpoint Popkin characterizes cyberbullying as the newest form of meanness, which in her opinion cannot be outlawed. Given what you know on the topic, do you agree that cyberbullying is merely meanness and as such cannot be made illegal, or do you view cyberbullying as more than simply mean behavior? Explain, citing examples from the viewpoints you have read in your answer.

Chapter 2

Should Cyberbullying Be a Criminal Offense?

Tina Meier holds pictures of her daughter, Megan, who committed suicide after being bullied on MySpace. Meier has been instrumental in the enactment of anti-cyberbullying legislation.

Cyberbullying Should Be Treated as a Crime

Linda T. Sanchez

> *"Prosecutors should have a tool at their disposal to allow them to punish [cyberbullies]."*

In the following viewpoint Linda T. Sanchez argues that cyberbullying should be made illegal. She discusses how there are grave consequences for the victims of cyberbullying—some of whom have ended up dead after being tormented by online bullies. Sanchez contends, however, that under the law there are no consequences for cyberbullies because cyberbullying is not yet illegal. She suggests that cyberbullying be treated as a crime punishable by law. Cyberbullying deserves to be treated as a criminal act, in her opinion, because of the toll it takes on young people's self-esteem and their mental and physical health. Sanchez thinks that making cyberbullying against the law would not violate free speech because threatening people—whether in person or over the Internet—is not a constitutionally protected form of expression. She concludes that because it can have

Linda T. Sanchez, "Testimony on 'Megan Meier Cyberbullying Prevention Act'," iCrime, Terrorism, and Homeland Security Subcommittee of the U.S. House Judiciary Committee, September 30, 2009.

such serious consequences, law enforcement officials should be able to prosecute cyberbullies under the law.

Sanchez is a Democratic congresswoman from California. She is the primary author of the Megan Meier Cyberbullying Prevention Act, which was introduced in 2009 and seeks to make cyberbullying illegal.

AS YOU READ, CONSIDER THE FOLLOWING QUESTIONS:
1. What were the legal implications of Lori Drew's cyberbullying, according to Sanchez?
2. What kinds of speech does the author say the Supreme Court has found acceptable to regulate under the First Amendment?
3. What forms of online speech does Sanchez say should remain legal?

When I was first elected to Congress, I held a series of meetings with local school superintendents and law enforcement leaders to learn more about the challenges they face in helping to keep our children safe and on the right track.

I heard a recurring theme—that bullying is not a harmless prank or rite of passage. It is dangerous, both physically and mentally.

Bullying can lead to poor school performance, more absences, or even dropping out of school altogether.

The prospect of assault and harassment can lead a child to join a gang for protection. Not only can bullying cause physical injuries, including cuts, bruises, and broken bones, but it can also lead to depression, and even suicide.

The New Face of Bullying

This is why I have been working to change federal law so that schools can use federal funds to address and prevent bullying and harassment.

But, over the last several years, I have learned that this approach isn't enough.

Bullying has gone electronic. It occurs in text messages and G-Chat [Google Chat]; on Facebook and MySpace; on cell phones and the internet.

This literally means that kids can be bullied any hour of the day or night and even in their own homes.

Today's kids are so wired into their electronic social networks that they type more messages than they speak each day. Their virtual world is more real to them than the so-called real world.

For those of us over 30, this can be difficult to comprehend. Let me give you an example to illustrate the problem.

Imagine if, in our day, a student brought a big TV out to the quad and played for the entire student body a video tape in which he threatened and harassed a second student. By the end of the day, everyone, and I mean everyone, would have seen or heard about it.

Well, that's exactly what cyberbullying is. Because of the anonymity and deception the internet allows, this form of bullying is particularly dangerous.

If Bobby posts a video on his Facebook page that harasses and threatens to rape and kill Ashley, that video isn't private. It's not buried on Bobby's profile page somewhere.

It's public. It appears when any of Bobby's Facebook friends log in—right there up front on their home page, so they can't miss it.

This story isn't just a hypothetical. It happened to a brave young woman named Hail Ketchum-Wiggins, who lives in Southern California, near my Congressional district.

Getting Away with Murder

And similar bullying incidents are happening every day to young people across our nation.

Cyberbullying is always mean, ill mannered, and cruel. But some cyberbullying is so harmful that it rises to the level of criminal behavior.

My bill, the Megan Meier Cyberbullying Prevention Act, is named to honor a young woman who was the victim of just such criminal behavior.

Three years ago [in 2006], 13-year-old Megan Meier of Missouri hung herself after being tormented and harassed by her 15-year-old

Megan Meier's mother, Tina, greets Missouri governor Matt Blunt after he signed a bill that will protect children from Internet harassment.

MySpace friend "Josh." "Josh" told her, among other things, "The world would be better off without you."

Eventually, Megan's family learned that "Josh" was really a creation of Lori Drew.

Local prosecutors in Missouri couldn't bring charges against Lori Drew because, at the time, Missouri had no law to punish such cruelty.

A federal prosecutor, in a similar bind, got creative and charged Drew with computer fraud. Even though the jury convicted her, the judge threw out the conviction.

The result is that Drew, an adult, and one who should have been setting an example of good behavior, will never be punished for her outrageous behavior toward her 13-year-old victim, Megan.

Making Cyberbullying a Crime

These are just brief examples of why Congress needs to address new crimes like cyberbullying.

Words that didn't exist just a couple of years ago, including "sexting" and "textual harassment," describe the new ways people use technology to hurt, harass, and humiliate each other. When these behaviors become serious, repeated, and hostile, we can no longer ignore them.

While Missouri has since enacted a cyberbullying statute, the children of other states are waiting for Congress to act. That is why I am grateful that the [House Judiciary] Committee is considering the Megan Meier Cyberbullying Prevention Act.

Before I conclude, I want to acknowledge how difficult it will be to craft a prohibition on cyberbullying that is consistent with the Constitution. But I also believe that working together for our children, we can and must do so.

The Supreme Court has already recognized that some regulation of speech is consistent with the First Amendment. For example, the Court has approved restrictions on true threats, obscenities, and some commercial speech. But it has been more hostile to attempts to limit political speech.

I do not intend anything in the Megan Meier Cyberbullying Prevention Act to override Supreme Court jurisprudence.

Instead, I want the law to be able to distinguish between an annoying chain email, a righteously angry political blog post, or a miffed text to an ex-boyfriend—all of which are and should remain legal—and serious, repeated, and hostile communications made with the intent to harm.

When the latter rises to a criminal level, as it did in the case of Lori Drew, prosecutors should have a tool at their disposal to allow them to punish the perpetrator.

I believe that we can protect our right to free speech and victims of cyberbullying at the same time.

I look forward to working with colleagues on both sides of the aisle [opposing political parties] to do so.

I thank you for the opportunity to testify today and hope that you will all join me in supporting this legislation.

EVALUATING THE AUTHORS' ARGUMENTS:

Linda T. Sanchez believes people who cyberbully others commit a crime. Timothy Birdnow, the author of the following viewpoint, believes that while cyberbullying is abhorrent behavior, there is no crime in it. After reading both viewpoints, what is your opinion on the criminal nature of cyberbullying? Should it be considered a crime or not? Explain your reasoning using evidence from the texts you have read.

Viewpoint

2

Cyberbullying Should Not Be Treated as a Crime

Timothy Birdnow

"There is no crime in cyberbullying."

In the following viewpoint, Timothy Birdnow explains why he thinks it is inappropriate to treat cyberbullying as a crime. Cyberbullying is nothing more than being mean to people online, says Birdnow. He discusses the case of Megan Meier, who killed herself after a woman named Lori Drew posed online as a teenage boy and tormented her. Birdnow says although Drew's behavior was reprehensible, there is nothing inherently criminal about it—Drew did not tell Meier to kill herself nor did she threaten her in any way; she simply acted like a jerk. Birdnow says the government cannot make it against the law for people to be mean to one another—it has no authority to do this nor is it the most effective way to reduce cyberbullying. He suggests a better way to reduce cyberbullying is to make it taboo, or looked down upon by society. He concludes that this has

Timothy Birdnow, "Cyberbullying Laws and the Moral Code," *American Thinker*, May 24, 2009. Copyright © American Thinker 2009. Reproduced by permission.

worked to curb other unpleasant behaviors in the past and is how society should deal with the problem of cyberbullying.

Timothy Birdnow is a conservative writer who lives and blogs in St. Louis, Missouri. His articles have appeared on the Internet sites Pajamas Media, Intellectual Conservative, Orthodoxy Today, and American Thinker.

AS YOU READ, CONSIDER THE FOLLOWING QUESTIONS:
1. In what way is Lori Drew like Al Capone, according to the author?
2. How might pro-life organizations and church groups suffer from a law against cyberbullying, according to Birdnow?
3. According to the author, how did saying "the N-word" become taboo?

When a jury convicted 49-year-old Lori Drew of O'Fallon, Missouri (an ex-urb of St. Louis) in the now-infamous cyber-bullying case in which Drew posed as a teenage boy on Myspace to woo—then harass—13 year old Megan Meier, many were pleased that justice was done. But that pleasure quickly turned to disgust when it was learned that the jury's verdict came with a standardized recommendation of probation and a large fine rather than jail time. The presiding judge in the case can still impose jail time at the sentencing hearing on May 18, [2009] and he is under considerable pressure to do so; the troubled young girl hanged herself as a result of Mrs. Drew's harassment.

Reprehensible Is Not Necessarily Criminal

But Lori Drew was convicted by a jury in Los Angeles, not in Missouri, because there were no laws in the Show-Me State against what she did. Much like [gangster] Al Capone, who was not convicted of racketeering or other criminal charges but of *tax evasion*, Drew could not be accused of any real crime, so Federal prosecutors charged her with fraud for creating a false profile on Myspace. Myspace is based in Beverly Hills.

And Mrs. Drew was acquitted of 3 felony counts because it could not be shown that she operated solely with malicious intent. She was convicted of 3 misdemeanor charges of unauthorized access to the networking site.

In short, there is no crime in cyberbullying.

But people want Megan's death avenged, and interviews after the announcement of the verdict were nearly universal; toss Drew in the dungeon and throw away the key!

The judge in this case will have to be brave to follow the recommended sentencing guidelines. [The judge acquitted her.]

But the question remains; should a reprehensible but legal act be punished with the force of law simply because we judge it to be a reprehensible act? I would argue that the Law is not God, and that sometimes justice should not be meted out by our guardians in government.

Being Mean Is Not a Crime

First, let me state unequivocally that a grown adult who would harass a 13-year-old girl is the worst sort of scum, deserving of near total ostracism by the community. She should also be subject to civil penalties should Megan's parents decide to sue. That said, I'm not at all sure it is a good idea to place the force of Law into this situation.

That the child in this instance died is not really pertinent to the discussion, insofar as it cannot be established that Drew intended to drive Megan Meier to commit suicide. Were Lori Drew's intentions malicious? Yes, of course, but malice alone isn't grounds for charging someone with a felony. There is no right in the Constitution to be free of verbal mistreatment from another citizen. There have been many, many instances throughout history of individuals harassing other individuals, and it has traditionally been understood that such treatment may be immoral but does not fall within the purview of the legal code.

> **FAST FACT**
>
> A study published in the March 2010 issue of the *Archives of Pediatric and Adolescent Medicine* found that in general, bullying is on the decline, down from 22 percent of kids reporting being bullied in 2003 to 15 percent being bullied in 2008.

It should also be pointed out that a computer can be turned off, or the victim of cyberbullying can take actions to block or otherwise avoid

Lori Drew leaves the federal courthouse in Los Angeles after a judge tentatively threw out her conviction for her role in a MySpace hoax that led to the suicide of thirteen-year-old Megan Meier.

dealing with such a situation. Steps can be taken (like restraining orders) to kick the bully off the network or whatnot. It is far easier to avoid cyberbullying than it is to avoid playground bullies; the playground bully is physically present, and can confront the victim directly.

Laws Cannot Stop Bullies

I am not trying to be hard-hearted here; I detest bullying in all forms. The problem is, authorities can *never* stop bullying in the long run; it is up to the victim herself to do that. Bullying is one of those unfortunate things that simply cannot be dealt with by others.

Which brings us to the purpose of this essay; contemporary America has an almost spiritual faith in the powers of government to redress all wrongs, and hard cases make bad law.

Which is why what Democrat Linda Sanchez [a congresswoman] is doing is so disturbing; the California Democrat has proposed a bill to make electronic harassment into a Federal felony, ostensibly to make cases like Megan Meier's fall within the authority of Federal prosecutors. . . .

What does it mean to coerce, intimidate, harass, or cause substantial emotional distress? Such wording opens a Pandora's box, because any sharp trial lawyer could claim that anything conveyed through electronic media is somehow intimidating, harassing, coercive, or distressing.

Even Offensive Speech Must Be Protected

Would pro-life organizations be guilty of violating this law for claiming abortion is murder? Would a Baptist church group be guilty if they say homosexuality is against God's law? For that matter, this very essay could be misconstrued as advocating bullying and thus be distressing.

This is another example of "never letting a crisis go to waste"; a very bad situation could be turned into a very useful tool for the [political] Left! The hard case that resulted in the suicide of a young girl can be manipulated to, say, shut the mouths of those who are opposed to his High Holiness [President] Barack Hussein Obama and Congregation.

The Constitution protects the freedom of individuals to speak as they see fit—including speech that is offensive. Often the "offensive" speech becomes the norm in future years. Consider the abolitionists;

this law could well have been used in antebellum [pre–Civil War] times (had they had computers and cell phones back then) to shut the abolitionists' mouths. Many considered them kooks and fire-brands, and slavery could well have never ended because government silenced their speech. . . .

Cyberbullying Should Be Taboo but Legal

America has made the N-word (note I do not even use it here) into a taboo, something that cannot be said in polite company. How did this happen? People used to use it with regularity up until the 1970's, and many black people still use it among themselves. What happened is that a majority of people decided it was a hateful, hurtful expression and so people themselves changed the public norm and made the word anathema. Anyone who uses that word suffers social scorn and ostracism, and so few continue to use it. Society, not law, made that word unacceptable.

And *that* is what must be done about cyberbullying. The new technology, the internet, text messaging, all of these things offer a degree of anonymity that give courage to those who would never have the nerve to say such things openly. The mouse becomes a lion when he can hide amid the millions of gigabytes coursing through the electronic nervous system. Couple this sense of anonymity with a culture that has coarsened, a culture where one is liberated from decent behavior, and you have a recipe for this very thing. It must become a matter of unacceptable ill-manners on the part of the average computer user—be they adult, teen, or tween. The law is simply inadequate for dealing with this sort in any but the most hamhanded—and ultimately restrictive—fashion. What happened to the N-word in polite society has to be applied to all forms of nasty commentary by computer users. . . .

But attempting to restrict such things through force alone is destined not just for failure but for an increase in such, because the standard then becomes the exercise of power over others rather than the exercise of restraint of one's own. To use the modern moral relativistic rejoinder "what right have you to judge me!" That right, that employment of the power of the State, becomes purely arbitrary. Instead of calling behavior like Lori Drew's immoral it becomes simply illegal—

something far weaker. People chafe under a code of behavior imposed from without, and the moral imperatives will become that much more despised.

EVALUATING THE AUTHOR'S ARGUMENTS:

Birdnow argues that characterizing cyberbullying as immoral will eradicate the behavior more effectively than characterizing it as illegal. In one to two paragraphs, explain what he means by this. Then, state whether or not you agree.

Laws Against Cyberbullying Are Needed

Ben Leichtling

In the following viewpoint, Ben Leichtling argues that anti-cyberbullying laws are needed to protect children from being harassed online. He says cyberbullying has become a very serious problem that affects thousands of kids on any given day. Education and anti-bullying programs are not enough to combat the problem—in his opinion, laws are needed that make cyberbullying an illegal, punishable crime. Leichtling says laws against cyberbullying would not threaten free speech. He acknowledges there would probably be some challenging cases in which it was hard to determine whether a person's online actions constituted harassment or free expression, but he is willing to accept such challenging cases if it means being allowed to prosecute the clear-cut ones. Leichtling reminds readers that the purpose of laws is to stop people from harming others—to this end, he concludes that laws are the best way to protect kids from cyberbullying.

> *"We do need Federal laws to stop cyber bullying, harassment and abuse."*

Ben Leichtling is a bullying expert and the creator of the Bullies Be Gone anti-bullying program.

AS YOU READ, CONSIDER THE FOLLOWING QUESTIONS:
1. What is the difference, according to Leichtling, between teaching people to behave civilly online and teaching people proper table manners?
2. According to the author, what is the purpose of a law?
3. What will people do if given the chance to seek power and revenge, according to Leichtling?

A ccording to the *Wall Street Journal* article, "CyberBullying Report Opposes Regulation," a recent report on cyberbullying suggests that, unlike other Internet scares, this one is well-founded, but it questions some of the regulatory efforts that are gathering steam. "The report, by the Progress & Freedom Foundation, a right-leaning Washington think tank that focuses on technology public policy, says that data from child-safety researchers" indicate that much of the furor is overblown.

I disagree strongly: The furor is not overblown and we do need Federal laws to stop cyber bullying, harassment and abuse.

Objections Make No Sense
The right-leaning think tank's objections to new anti-cyber bullying laws are that:

Worries over online predators are overblown because one study of arrests from 2000 to 2006 showed that most of the offenders approached undercover investigators, not kids. I'm glad the offenders approached undercover investigators. But that's no reason not to have laws. Between 2006 and now, offenders have gotten smarter. And, of course we want laws so we can protect the kids who are approached.

They estimate that threats due to peer-to-peer bullying are more serious that those due to cyber bullying. Even if that's true, that's no reason to abandon kids who are targets of cyber bullying, harassment and abuse. As shown by the case of Lori Drew, without Federal laws, cyber bullies can't be prosecuted effectively. The Judge acquitted this

New Jersey senator Robert Menendez speaks during a press conference about new federal legislation to educate children and teens about the dangers of cyberbullying through the SAFE Internet Act.

adult even though she set up the MySpace site that was used to harass and abuse teenager Megan Meier until she committed suicide.

Laws Discourage Bad Behavior

Laws pose "thorny issues" that are entwined with free speech. Again, that's no reason not to enter the thicket. That simply lets us know that the laws will have gray areas and both the law and the interpretations will be continuously evolving as hardened criminals find loopholes. Laws encourage angry, potentially vindictive people to think twice before doing anything impulsive and rash.

Laws would make statements that defame, embarrass, harm, abuse, threaten, slander or harass third parties illegal online, even though such statements would be allowed if said on a playground. That's not a problem; that's an obvious benefit. That acknowledges the truism that statements made in a local context or face-to-face usually have very different consequences than hostility put out to the whole world on the internet, especially if the statements are anonymous or made through the safety of false identities.

Education Alone Is Not Enough

We can solve the problem best through better education. Nonsense. Of course, education and vigorous stop-bullies programs are very helpful, but they're not enough. Education alone does not yield the most benefits. Education, anti-bullying programs and enforced laws all together yield the most benefits.

Teaching people to behave civilly online is no different than teaching children to use proper table manners, to cover their mouths when they sneeze or to say "thank you." That's also nonsense. If an adult is a slob at home, no one else is harmed. If someone gets drunk and disruptive at a restaurant, a movie theater or a ball game, they can be asked to leave or ejected or arrested. The harm caused by eating with the wrong fork or not saying "please" or "thank you" is minor compared to the harm that can be caused by cyber bullying, harassment or abuse. Ask the families of Megan Meier or Jessica Logan, both of whom committed suicide after they were made the targets of cyber bullying. Ask the families of the thousands we don't hear about . . . in the media. They suffer, helpless to stop their abusers, but valiantly and quietly to struggle through life.

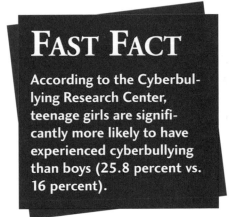

FAST FACT

According to the Cyberbullying Research Center, teenage girls are significantly more likely to have experienced cyberbullying than boys (25.8 percent vs. 16 percent).

Laws Can Protect Kids

Online attacks are becoming an epidemic. Some sites even specialize as forums for anonymous bashing and attacks.

Laws are made to state the standards to which we aspire and to diminish people's ability to harm others as much as possible. Laws may be imperfect and enforcement may be difficult and spotty, but that's better than nothing. I'd rather have anti-bullying laws that protect kids 90% of the time and have difficulties 10% of the time, than have no laws to stop cyber bullying and leave kids vulnerable 100% of the time.

Girls Especially Suffer from Cyberbullying

Polls show that girls—specifically, older girls—are more likely to suffer from cyberbullying than boys are.

Online Rumors Tend to Target Girls		
Have you, personally, ever experienced any of the following things online?	**Boys**	**Girls**
Someone taking a private e-mail, IM (instant message), or text message you sent them and forwarding it to someone else or posting it where others could see it	13%	17%
Someone sending you a threatening or aggressive e-mail, IM, or text message	10%	15%
Someone spreading a rumor about you online	9%	16%
Someone posting an embarrassing picture of you online without your permission	5%	7%
At least one of the forms of cyberbullying listed above	23%	36%

Older Girls Are the Group Most Likely to Report Experiencing Some Form of Cyberbullying	
Girls 15–17	41%
Boys 15–17	29%
Girls 12–14	34%
Boys 12–14	22%

Taken from: Amanda Lenhart, "Data Memo: Cyberbullying and Online Teens," Pew Internet & American Life Project, June 27, 2007 and "Parents and Teens Survey," October–November 2006.

Our laws and even our system of checks and balances are founded on our understanding that no matter how much education people have, they will often seek power and revenge. They won't always be good and sweet and kind. If given the chance, people will be mean, nasty and vicious to others, especially if they can act anonymously or the target can't fight back effectively.

We must rise to the challenge posed by new technology and keep evolving laws and enforcing them the best we can. We must stop cyber bullying.

EVALUATING THE AUTHORS' ARGUMENTS:

A key point of Leichtling's argument is that laws can help reduce the extent to which people are mean and nasty to one another. How do you think each of the other authors represented in this chapter would respond to this idea? Write one or two sentences for each author, then state your opinion on the matter.

Laws Against Cyberbullying Threaten Individual Liberty

Michele Catalano

"Any Internet user now risks criminal proceedings for doing something as simple as creating a fake name to post messages on a website, something many people do each day for legitimate reasons."

Laws against cyberbullying threaten free speech and liberty, argues Michele Catalano in the following viewpoint. She discusses the case of Lori Drew, a woman who posed as a teenage boy online and harassed Megan Meier, her daughter's classmate, until Meier killed herself. Catalano argues that although Drew's behavior was abhorrent, it was not illegal since Drew never personally threatened Meier. Catalano says all Drew is really guilty of is creating a fake online profile and of being mean. But outlawing such behavior would instantly criminalize thousands, even millions of Internet users who use fake online names for legitimate reasons. It would also make it illegal for people to write anything offensive on the Internet, which Catalano says they are allowed to do under the First Amendment, which protects free speech. For all of these reasons Catalano thinks laws are not the appropriate way to reduce cyberbullying.

Michele Catalano is a writer and photographer who lives on Long Island, New York.

AS YOU READ, CONSIDER THE FOLLOWING QUESTIONS:

1. Who is Josh Evans and how does he factor into the author's argument?
2. Of what crime was Lori Drew found guilty, according to Catalano?
3. In what legitimate ways do people use fake names online, according to the author?

Everyone loves when justice is served. But sometimes what looks like justice is just a façade—and a dangerous one at that.

Take the case of Lori Drew. Drew is a 49-year-old mother of two from Missouri whose MySpace prank resulted in the suicide of 13-year-old Megan Meier.

Megan, like most girls her age, had a MySpace account. Megan was having some emotional troubles. She considered herself overweight, had very low self-esteem, and was depressed enough to have had suicidal thoughts. But that all changed when she met a 16-year-old boy on MySpace. Josh Evans paid attention to her and made her smile. Their friendship blossomed and became somewhat romantic, in a teenage sort of way. Then very suddenly, everything turned sour. Josh became mean and nasty to Megan, and began messaging her school friends saying terrible things about her. The friends ganged up on Megan and posted hurtful comments on her MySpace page. Then Josh wrote to her: "Everybody in O'Fallon [her town] knows how you are. You are a bad person and everybody hates you. Have a shitty rest of your life. The world would be a better place without you." A distraught Megan then hung herself. She died the next day.

Sadly, the boy Megan ended her life over never even existed. Lori Drew, the mother of Megan's former best friend, created "Josh Evans" for the sole purpose of interfering in her daughter's social life. Drew claims she started the charade just to see if Megan was saying anything about her daughter on MySpace. Why it became mean, cruel, and vicious is something only she knows. She has made excuses for her actions, but none that excuse the abhorrent behavior that literally crushed Megan's spirit and led to her suicide. A grown woman posted messages as a teenage boy, saying hurtful, horrible things to a 13-year-old girl that she knew was suffering from depression to begin with. How did she know? Because Megan went on vacations with that family. They knew she took medication. She was the best friend of their daughter. And yet this mother decided to interfere in her daughter's life to the extent that she became a part of, and a cause of, so much teenage drama.

There were immediate cries for justice and punishment. Someone needed to be held responsible for Megan's death and the public outcry indicated that they wanted Lori Drew's head. But did she commit a crime? While her actions were certainly despicable and vile, were they criminal?

Making Normal Internet Use Illegal

According to the U.S. Department of Justice, that answer is yes. Exploiting an anti-hacking law, a federal grand jury [in May 2008] returned a

Defense attorney for Lori Drew, H. Dean Steward, talks to the press about Drew's misdemeanor federal conviction in the Megan Meier cyberbullying case. The conviction was later overturned.

four count indictment against Drew: one count of conspiracy and three counts of accessing protected computers without authorization. Because Drew could not be legally tried for her part in the death of Meier, she was tried instead for breaking cyber-laws, namely, breaking the MySpace Terms of Service.

Would there have been such a rush to judgment had the case not received nationwide attention? The swell of Internet postings on this story grew to such large proportions that mainstream news eventually picked it up. At that point, it seemed like justice was almost demanded; people were calling for the head of Lori Drew and, even though there was no way to physically tie her to the death of Megan Meier, the authorities made sure that such a public case was going to come to its proper conclusion: with justice served.

But the cost of that justice is too high to pay. What Drew's indictment means, in essence, is that any Internet user now risks criminal proceedings for doing something as simple as creating a fake name to post messages on a website, something many people do each day for legitimate reasons.

A Moral Crime, Not a Legal One

Yes, perhaps Lori Drew did commit a crime, but it was more of a moral crime, not a legal one. Indicting someone because their words and actions led another person to kill themselves is opening a Pandora's Box of trouble. Unfortunately, in this cruel world things like this happen every day, particularly when teenagers are involved. The fact that Lori Drew used the Internet as a tool to perpetrate her viciousness is the only thing that is giving anyone any authority to prosecute her.

If her words to Megan were spoken, or written on a note tacked to the Meiers' door, would there be the same outrage? Would Lori Drew be facing jail time, presumably for her complicity in Megan's death? Probably not, because there is no law to loophole that says you can't leave a fictitious note from a nonexistent person on someone's door.

Punishing Everyday Internet Users

By turning MySpace into the victim and using the hacker law to prosecute Drew, are we now to understand that we can't make fictitious profiles or user names on Internet forums? That thousands of people who don't want their employees to read their blogs or their exes to find them can no longer hide behind a pen name, even if there is no criminal intent to using that name? Are we going to have to state our intent when creating profiles or email addresses? After all, it is inconsistent to prosecute one person for this action and not the thousands upon thousands of people who practice this daily.

As a parent of teenage kids, I'm sympathetic to the Meier family and align myself with those who wish to see some kind of punishment served on Lori Drew for being intentionally mean to a child she knew was vulnerable and depressed. A good, old-fashioned public shunning comes to mind.

However, handing down a verdict using laws meant to keep the Internet safe from hackers is doing a vast injustice to the well-being of the Internet and will do nothing to keep our children safe from cyberharassment. As parents, it is our job to teach our children how to properly use the Internet and to set guidelines for them. We cannot ask the government to step in and virtually tie the hands of thousands of users in order to protect our children from vicious bullies like Lori Drew.

EVALUATING THE AUTHOR'S ARGUMENTS:

Catalano warns that laws that criminalize certain kinds of online activity will end up being used to punish thousands of innocent Internet users. Do you agree with her that cyberbullying laws could have this effect? Why or why not? Cite evidence from the viewpoints you have read in your answer.

Chapter 3

How Can Cyberbullying Be Prevented?

Often the best way to defend oneself from cyber-bullying is to tell a parent or school administrator about it.

Lawsuits May Prevent Cyberbullying

Jonathan Turley

"Litigation could succeed in forcing schools to take bullying more seriously."

In the following viewpoint, Jonathan Turley argues that lawsuits may help reduce cyberbullying. He discusses how bullying has become an increasingly serious problem, rendering its victims emotionally and physically scarred and sometimes even dead. Turley points out that bullying often turns criminal—it is against the law to threaten, beat up, paralyze, or kill other people, yet this is exactly what bullies do to their victims. In his opinion, lawsuits against this behavior may help protect innocent children from being harmed. By incapacitating them as children, Turley says lawsuits can also prevent bullies from continuing their criminal activity into adulthood. Turley concludes that schools need to be forced to take bullying more seriously.

Jonathan Turley is a law professor at the George Washington University in Washington, D.C.

Jonathan Turley, "Bullying's Day in Court," *USA Today*, July 15, 2008. Reproduced by permission of the author.

AS YOU READ, CONSIDER THE FOLLOWING QUESTIONS:

1. Who is Billy Wolfe and how does he factor into the author's argument?
2. What did a 2008 study by the Rochester Institute of Technology, cited by Turley, find about victims of cyberbullying?
3. What percentage of bullies does the author say have at least one criminal conviction by the age of twenty-four?

Mathew Mumbauer, 11, never saw it coming. One moment in early March [2008], he was walking down the stairs at Brickett Elementary School in Lynn, Mass. The next moment he was lying at the bottom of the stairs. He was left paralyzed and on a ventilator. Mathew's parents blame bullies who had been hounding Mathew for most of the year.

Mathew is only the latest victim of bullying in our schools, and some parents are turning from the schoolhouse to the courthouse to seek relief. Meanwhile, tens of thousands of students are anxiously counting down the days left in summer and the approach of another bullying season.

With the advent of the Internet, YouTube and MySpace, bullying is becoming more prevalent and more lethal—allowing bullies to move from playgrounds to cyberspace in pursuit of their prey. While the number of bullying lawsuits is unknown, some high-profile cases are focusing attention on the national problem.

> **FAST FACT**
>
> About half of all Nevada students have been targeted by cyberbullies. For this reason, in July 2010 Nevada made cyberbullying a crime. District attorneys can charge those who cyberbully with a misdemeanor offense that is punishable with jail time; schools can also suspend or otherwise discipline cyberbullies.

Dealing with bullies has long been treated as just part of "growing up," a natural and even maturing element of childhood. Encounters with the ubiquitous bully in movies and in literature are treated as a

Nineteen States Have Anti-Cyberbullying Legislation

Nineteen states have some type of anti-cyberbullying law. This chart shows which states make cyberbullying against the law and what kinds of actions are prosecutable.

Definitions		
State	Amends previous law to include electronic communication	Bullying is illegal on school property or at school-sponsored events and/or use of data or computer software accessed through school computer systems
Arkansas	X	X
California	X	
Delaware	X	X
Florida	X	X
Idaho	X	
Iowa	X	
Kansas	X	X
Maryland	X	X
Minnesota	X	
Missouri	X	X
Nebraska	X	X
New Jersey	X	X
Oklahoma	X	X
Oregon	X	X
Pennsylvania	X	X
Rhode Island	X	X
South Carolina	X	X
Utah	X	
Washington	X	

Location of Cyberbullying				
State	Does not apply to off-campus bullying	Applies whether or not electronic communication originated at school or through school equipment	Law did not specify whether schools can discipline off-campus cyberbullying	School can define bullying to include off-campus cyberbullying
Arkansas		X		
California				
Delaware				X
Florida				
Idaho			X	
Iowa			X	
Kansas			X	
Maryland			X	
Minnesota				
Missouri				
Nebraska	X			
New Jersey				
Oklahoma		X		
Oregon			X	
Pennsylvania				X
Rhode Island			X	
South Carolina			X	
Utah				
Washington			X	

Taken from: "Legislation on Cyberbullying," Iowa Policy Research Organization, University of Iowa, October 2009, p.4.

type of rite of passage, particularly for boys. From "the Ogre" in *Revenge of the Nerds* to Scut Farkas in *A Christmas Story*, the bullies always lose when you simply stand up to them, right?

Perhaps, or you can end up dead. Across the country, schoolchildren have been killed after standing up to bullies in places as wideranging as West Paducah, Ky., Edinboro, Pa., and Jonesboro, Ark.

Turning Children into Prey

Being a bully remains a popular choice for students, particularly in middle schools, where bullying often peaks. A 2004 survey by KidsHealth found that 40% of children from 9- to 13-years-old admitted to bullying. Another recent study prepared for the American Psychological Association showed that 80% of middle school students admitted to bullying behavior in the prior 30 days. Like Piggy in *Lord of the Flies*, a child can become a collective target—the object of a natural juvenile inclination to subordinate and isolate individuals. Just ask 15-year-old Billy Wolfe in Fayetteville, Ark.

At some point, high school bullies made him a type of collective sport prey. They even filmed the hunt. One video shows a boy spontaneously announcing that he is going to beat up Billy Wolfe in front of Billy's younger sister, walking up and punching him at a bus stop.

Billy's beatings were triggered years ago after his mom complained to the parents of a bully. The next day, the boy presented Billy with a list of 20 names of boys who signed up to beat him up. Attacks would occur at any time and any place—the bathroom, shop class, the school bus—with one requiring that Billy receive medical treatment.

This is not the first lawsuit involving Fayetteville and bullying. The district was previously sued after a student was savagely beaten for being gay. In a similar case in Kansas City, Kan., a jury awarded Dylan Theno $250,000 against the Tonganoxie School District for years of bullying due to the false rumor that he was gay.

As the suicide of 13-year-old Megan Meier showed the nation, Internet sites such as MySpace have opened up new opportunities for cyberbullying. Megan's suicide was allegedly triggered by an adult neighbor, Lori Drew, pretending to be a 16-year-old boy who not only dumped her but also initiated a cyberpile-on by other kids. A 2008 study of more than 40,000 adolescents by the Rochester Institute

Viewpoint author and constitutional law expert Jonathan Turley believes that more anti-cyberbullying laws are needed to protect children against threats and physical harm from bullies.

of Technology revealed that 59% of cybervictims in grades seven to nine were bullied by kids whom they knew.

Bullies Often Turn Criminal

The social costs of bullying are often ignored. A federal study found that 60% of boys who were bullies in middle school had at least one criminal conviction by the age of 24. Bullying is also routinely tied to suicide attempts, drug abuse, and drop-outs, or worse, violence by the victims.

In Littleton, Colo., the killers at Columbine High School in 1999 had complained about being bullied. In Hoover, La., Felicia Reynolds sued the school district after her son, Ricky, stood up to an alleged bully named Sean Joyner after years of complaints to officials at Hoover High School. After being removed from the school due to a separate incident, Sean was allowed to return and fought with Ricky. Sean died from a knife wound, and Ricky was put away for 20 years. Unlike the Hollywood formula of bully movies, when the Karate Kid in real life stands up to bully Johnny Lawrence, he ends up doing one to five years in the county jail.

Bullying Needs to Be Taken More Seriously

While many will chafe at the notion of moving from hall monitors to personal injury lawyers, litigation could succeed in forcing schools to take bullying more seriously.

The first step, however, is to dispense with the image of bullies as mere Scut Farkases waiting to be challenged and conquered. Bullies are not adverse object lessons for an educational system; they are the very antithesis of education. They are no more a natural part of learning than is parental abuse a natural part of growing up. That is one lesson Mathew Mumbauer learned all too well.

EVALUATING THE AUTHOR'S ARGUMENTS:

To make his argument, Turley tells the stories of Mathew Mumbauer, Billy Wolfe, Megan Meier, Sean Joyner, and Ricky Reynolds. In one to two sentences, summarize each of these people's stories and how they are used by Turley to support his argument. Did the use of these stories add a human element that helped convince you to agree with Turley that laws can prevent cyberbullying? Why or why not?

Education Can Help Prevent Cyberbullying

Nick Abrahams with Victoria Dunn

"Currently, the most effective weapons for combating cyber-bullying are education programs."

Creating laws against cyberbullying is not the best way to address the problem, argue Nick Abrahams and Victoria Dunn in the following viewpoint. Although the authors see cyberbullying as a growing and serious problem, they contend that laws are an ineffective way to stop it. In their opinion, cyberbullying is too subjective a crime to legislate—in other words, cyberbullying takes so many different forms, it would be impossible to craft a law and punishment that equitably covers all of them. In addition, the authors say that policing cyberbullying would be a futile task, since online content is constantly being put up and taken down. Furthermore, Abrahams and Dunn say cyberbullies are too young to be prosecuted by law—they think it would be inappropriate to throw children in jail or haul them before judges. A better approach to the problem, say the authors, is to create cyberbullying awareness programs that educate people on the dangers of cyberbullying and why and how they should avoid it.

Cyber-bullying is back in the spotlight. Earlier this month [May 2009] the [Australian] federal government announced it had established a Youth Advisory Group, consisting of young Australians, to advise it on cyber-bullying and other online issues.

Within a week came the report that two year 9 [ninth grade] students had been forced to leave a Sydney girls' school for cyber-bullying. As a result, I have been asked a number of times—shouldn't there be laws to stop this?

The answer is that there are some laws which cover the most aggressive forms of cyber-bullying but, unless you want to start filling jails with 15-year-olds, criminal sanctions are not the answer.

Cyberbullying Has Unique Challenges

Bullying has been around for a long time. Recently, many schools have really focused on the issue and there has been some success in reducing the incidence of traditional school yard bullying. However, the internet is the bully's new school yard. Studies have shown that cyber-bullying is widespread, with at least one in three teenagers the victim of cyber-bullying.

Cyber-bullying presents new challenges to young people, their parents and society. Cyber-bullying is different to traditional bullying in a number of key respects:

1. Anonymity: The impression of anonymity in the online world leads young people to feel less accountable for their actions and provides a false bravado to would-be bullies. In fact, a recent study has shown that, of bullies surveyed, 70 per cent had engaged only in cyber-bullying.

2. Geography: Rather than being limited to the school-yard, cyber-bullying operates wherever a young person uses the internet or a mobile phone. There are few areas of a young person's life which cyber-bullying cannot penetrate.

3. Impact: The internet provides a means to make bullying comments available to a wider audience than ever before. Through social networking sites, comments can be viewed by potentially thousands of people. The impact of and embarrassment caused by these statements is therefore magnified.

4. Permanence: Verbal comments are fleeting. Online they stay around, potentially forever.

Laws Already Exist

Where cyber-bullying is serious, it may be appropriate for the law to step in to impose penalties on bullies.

In cases where bullying involves a threat to kill or seriously injure a person, state-based criminal legislation could be used to lay criminal charges against bullies. However, where bullying does not include such threats, but is more in the realm of emotional cruelty, legal protection offered to victims is piecemeal.

A school cyberbully awareness program teaches anti-bullying therapy through expression.

Under the NSW [New South Wales] Crimes Act it is a criminal offence to harass or intimidate a school student while the student is at school. This offence can be applied to traditional off-line bullying, but has its limits as it applies only to activities done at school.

As cyber-bullying can occur exclusively outside the school yard, it is quite possible that cyber-bullying would not be caught by this provision.

The Commonwealth Criminal Code sets out an offence of using a carriage service (such as a mobile phone service or the internet) in a way that is menacing, harassing or offensive. The maximum penalty for committing the offence is 3 years imprisonment.

While it has the potential to be used in cases of cyber-bullying, to date charges under this section of the Code have been brought only in relation to harassing phone calls.

Some state governments have specifically expanded the scope of the off-line harassment laws to cover online activities.

In Victoria, for example, the stalking provisions of the Crimes Act could extend to catch cyber-bullies who post information about a victim on the internet, intending the post to cause mental harm to the victim, or to cause the victim to fear for his or her safety.

However, even where specific legislation designed to apply to such online activities exists it has been of little effect, with no cases of successful prosecution for cyber-bullying in Australia.

In the absence of specific and effective laws dealing with cyber-bullying, victims must rely on laws largely designed to apply in the off-line world and, in many cases, developed before the advent of the internet.

Such laws include defamation law (which may offer some redress to victims about whom false statements have been published online) and laws preventing harassment of individuals on the basis of race, religion and sexual orientation.

Too Subjective to Legislate

This piecemeal legal regime does not offer a comprehensive response to the increasing problem of cyber-bullying—nor should it.

Given the subjectivity of bullying, and the young age of many cyber-bullies, the traditional legal approach of deterring potential offenders by threatening criminal sanctions is not appropriate, except in the most serious cases.

There are those that propose that there should be laws requiring Internet Service Providers [ISPs] to remove bullying-related material from websites. While I am sympathetic to why people would want this, it is very difficult to create a workable solution.

How is the ISP to judge what is bullying content and what is not?

It is so subjective and places a heavy burden on ISPs. This issue of take down will become more acute in the future as more people seek to change their digital footprints—not just because of bullying material but perhaps because the content might be defamatory, or just something they wish a friend didn't put up on the internet when everyone was 18 or even something they themselves wish they did not put up on the internet when they were 18.

Education Is More Effective

Currently, the most effective weapons for combating cyber-bullying are education programs and a commitment by schools to implement and enforce policies. Such education programs should include:

- continuing education of teachers and schools about changes in technology and the potential for technology to be used by cyber-bullies;
- educating kids about cyber-bullying—why not to do it and how to deal with it; and
- educating parents about technology so they can understand what their kids are doing online and talk to them about it.

Bullying happens, but it should not be accepted as inevitable. Much has been done by schools and parents in recent years to raise awareness of and to reduce off-line bullying. This has been achieved without resorting to specific off-line bullying laws. Similarly, cyber-bullying needs to be targeted and stopped at the grass roots level.

The law should be there to backstop schools and parents in the most serious of cases. But new laws may become necessary depending on how cyber-bullying develops. Technology magnifies the potential for harm to be inflicted in ways we had not before imagined.

Remember the recent Lori Drew case. Who would have thought that a mother would make up a fictitious boy on MySpace, use the "boy" to court one of her teenage daughter's friends, then drop her coldly, causing the girl to commit suicide. Only in America—or maybe not.

EVALUATING THE AUTHORS' ARGUMENTS:

Abrahams and Dunn argue that cyberbullies are just kids who are too young to be thrown in jail or otherwise put through the criminal justice system for their actions. How might Jonathan Turley, author of the previous viewpoint, respond to this argument?

Stricter School Policies Can Prevent Cyberbullying

Jeanne Kohl-Welles

"By requiring our schools to include cyberbullying among the forms of harassment that schools must address through policies, we can educate our youth about its insidious effects."

In the following viewpoint, Jeanne Kohl-Welles argues that schools need to adopt stricter policies against cyberbullying. Cyberbullying is a serious and growing problem, she contends, and the majority of students have either bullied someone online or been the victim of cyberbullying. These actions drive students to depression and even suicide, she maintains. Kohl-Welles argues that just as schools are responsible for taking action against bullies who roam their hallways and schoolyards, so too must they act when their students are bullied online. Kohl-Welles recommends that schools adopt policies that prohibit cyberbullying against any student and make information available to students and parents about the seriousness of cyberbullying. She also recommends that electronic acts of harassment be added to school policies regarding illegal student behavior.

Jeanne Kohl-Welles, "Dealing with Cyberbullies," *Seattle Times*, January 19, 2006. Copyright © 2006 The Seattle Times Company. Reproduced by permission of the author.

Jeanne Kohl-Welles is a Washington state senator who has served on the state's Senate Early Learning, K–12 and Higher Education Committee.

AS YOU READ, CONSIDER THE FOLLOWING QUESTIONS:
1. According to I-SAFE America as cited by the author, what percentage of students have admitted to saying mean or hurtful things about their peers online?
2. In what way does Kohl-Welles say the anonymous nature of the Internet makes cyberbullying especially devastating for kids?
3. How does what happened to a student from Thurston County, Washington, factor into the author's argument?

"Sticks and stones may break my bones, but words will never hurt me."

These words were never true when baby boomers uttered them decades ago on playgrounds across America, and they are no more true now.

Instead, there are even more ways for today's youth to intimidate each other, thanks to cellphones and the Internet.

In classrooms and in bedrooms, teens text-message each other with an ease that amazes their parents. Yet, used maliciously, the technology that brings friends and families together can also deeply wound.

Cyberbullying—the use of e-mail, instant messaging, Web sites, camera phones and the like to torment someone—is on the rise. And with more children using this technology—and at an increasingly younger age—the problem shows no signs of abating.

Schools Need Aggressive Response

[Washington State] Senate Bill 5849 would add electronic acts to the definition of bullying, intimidation and harassment; under current law, school districts are required to have policies prohibiting such behavior toward a student. The legislation . . . also would require that schools make available to students and parents information on the seriousness of cyberbullying and the options that are available if a student is being so bullied.

The Effect of Cyberbullying on Its Victims

Polls show that girls are more likely to react to cyberbullying than boys are. Elementary and middle school students react more to cyberbullying than high schoolers.

The Effects on Males and Females

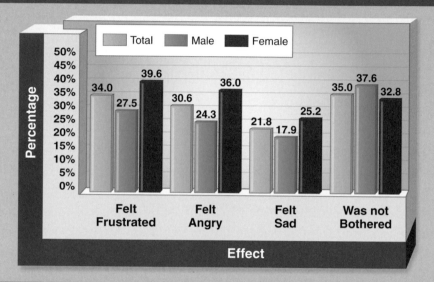

The Effects on Different Age Groups

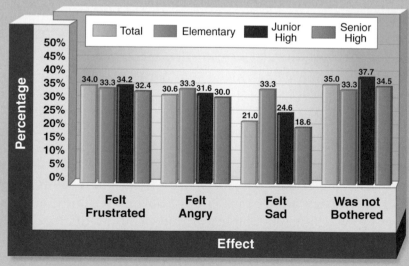

Taken from: Sameer Hinduja and Justin W. Patchin, "Cyberbullying Research Summary: Emotional and Psychological Consequences," Cyberbullying Research Center, 2009, 1–2.

And many students are. A study was recently conducted by I-SAFE America, an organization that promotes Web safety. Of the 1,500 students in fourth through eighth grades who were surveyed, 42 percent said they had been bullied online. And 53 percent fessed up to saying something mean or hurtful online. A majority—58 percent—had not told their parents that something upsetting had happened to them online.

Anonymity Makes It Worse

The anonymity of cyberspace is a powerful attraction for youth. Not having to take responsibility for caustic comments lulls the aggressor into thinking that there will be no repercussions. With estimates that up to half of the children online are there without parental supervision, the boundaries of good taste and appropriate language aren't necessarily being learned.

The 24/7 nature of the Internet means that youth can be victimized at any time—and anonymously at that. While it's hard enough to face your tormentor on the playground or in the lunchroom, imagine not knowing whom to confront when nasty words or vile rumors are spread about you.

"Everyone Hates Her"

One of the most compelling letters I have received as a legislator came from a mother in Virginia. She wrote that her teenage daughter had been the victim of cyberbullying for the previous three months, when several of her former girlfriends began posting malicious and hateful comments on a Web site.

Meetings with the school district brought no results. Even reports filed with the police department were futile. The mother shared that her daughter "has been told to move, that no one wants her here and that everyone hates her."

A teacher at Olsen Middle School in Dania Beach, Florida, directs a student in an anti-bullying program.

As a mother myself, my heart ached when I read that she was seeking emergency professional assistance that day for her daughter, who had started voicing suicidal thoughts. She asked for a copy of my bill to give to her own legislators.

Schools Need to Monitor Internet Use

No one should be victimized as this girl was. She was fortunate to have loving and concerned parents to advocate for her and to seek help. But there are others who have no one to turn to and so are left to suffer in silence. Their self-esteem eroded, their sense of personal safety violated, these young people often struggle in school and at home while they are victimized.

Last year [2005], a high-school student from Thurston County who was serving as a Senate page told me of having received e-mail death threats; another student had viewed her Web site and sent the threatening messages anonymously.

She filed a complaint with her local police department and the threats stopped. In addition to being extremely disturbing, the experience took considerable time to resolve—time that a teenager should be spending with friends and studying, not with law enforcement.

We can and should address this problem. By requiring our schools to include cyberbullying among the forms of harassment that schools must address through policies, we can educate our youth about its insidious effects. Just as bullies in the hallway must be stopped, so should those who use electronic means to torment others.

EVALUATING THE AUTHORS' ARGUMENTS:

Kohl-Welles is a Democratic state senator from Washington. Jimmy Wales, one of the authors of the following viewpoint, is the founder of Wikipedia. Does knowing these authors' backgrounds influence your opinion of their arguments? Why or why not? In what way do you think a person's credentials affect their credibility when it comes to making persuasive arguments?

Establishing an Online Code of Civility Can Prevent Cyberbullying

Jimmy Wales and Andrea Weckerle

"We [must] prevent the worst among us from silencing the best among us with hostility and incivility."

In the following viewpoint, Jimmy Wales and Andrea Weckerle argue that when online, Americans need to treat each other civilly, the same way they do when they are face-to-face. Wales and Weckerle discuss how people have used the Internet to slander and harass each other in ways they would never do in the real world. The anonymity of the Internet, along with its ease of use, seems to bring out the nasty side in people, but Wales and Weckerle say this is no excuse for treating each other poorly. They recommend all Internet users make concerted efforts to treat each other well online. They say users should ignore gossip Web sites and show each other that online hostility will not be tolerated. Wales and Weckerle conclude that the Internet can fulfill its potential as one of the greatest advances in human knowledge and communication only if people use it respectfully.

Wales is the founder of the online encyclopedia *Wikipedia* and sits on the board of CiviliNation, a nonprofit organization of which Weckerle is the founder and president.

AS YOU READ, CONSIDER THE FOLLOWING QUESTIONS:
1. What two specific examples of Internet hostility do the authors offer?
2. What does the term *media literacy* mean in the context of the viewpoint?
3. What kind of national support network do Wales and Weckerle recommend be created to deal with victims of online hostility?

I n less than 20 years, the World Wide Web has irrevocably expanded the number of ways we connect and communicate with others. This radical transformation has been almost universally praised.

What hasn't kept pace with the technical innovation is the recognition that people need to engage in civil dialogue. What we see regularly on social networking sites, blogs and other online forums is behavior that ranges from the carelessly rude to the intentionally abusive.

The Internet Encourages Meanness

Flare-ups occur on social networking sites because of the ease by which thoughts can be shared through the simple press of a button. Ordinary people, celebrities, members of the media and even legal professionals have shown insufficient restraint before clicking send. There is no shortage of examples—from the recent Twitter heckling at a Web 2.0 Expo in New York, to a Facebook poll asking whether President [Barack] Obama should be killed.

The comments sections of online gossip sites, as well as some national media outlets, often reflect semi-literate, vitriolic remarks that appear to serve no purpose besides disparaging their intended target. Some sites exist solely as a place for mean-spirited individuals to congregate and spew their venomous verbiage.

Online hostility targeting adults is vastly underreported. The reasons victims fail to come forward include the belief that online hostility is an unavoidable and even acceptable mode of behavior; the pervasive

Cyberbullying can be eliminated if people adhere to the same civility online as they do in face-to-face situations.

notion that hostile online speech is a tolerable form of free expression; the perceived social stigma of speaking out against attacks; and the absence of readily available support infrastructure to assist victims.

Establishing Cybercivility

The problem of online hostility, in short, shows no sign of abating on its own. Establishing cybercivility will take a concerted effort. We can start by taking the following steps:

First, and most importantly, we need to create an online culture in which every person can participate in an open and rational exchange of ideas and information without fear of being the target of unwarranted abuse, harassment or lies. Everyone who is online should have a sense of accountability and responsibility.

Too frequently, we hear the argument that being online includes the right to be nasty—and that those who choose to participate on the Web should develop thicker skin. This gives transgressors an out for immoral behavior.

Just as we've learned what is deemed appropriate face-to-face communication, we need to learn what is appropriate behavior in an environment

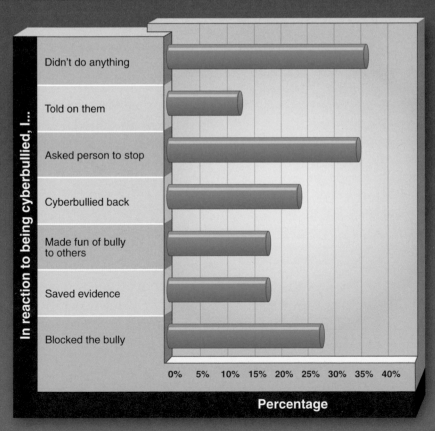

How Cyberbullying Victims React

The single greatest response to being cyberbullied is to do nothing. Because so many victims think nothing can be done, parents, educators, politicians, and students themselves have called for large-scale action to be taken to curb cyberbullying.

Reactions of Victims to Cyberbullying

In reaction to being cyberbullied, I...

- Didn't do anything
- Told on them
- Asked person to stop
- Cyberbullied back
- Made fun of bully to others
- Saved evidence
- Blocked the bully

0% 5% 10% 15% 20% 25% 30% 35% 40%

Percentage

Taken from: R. Kowalski and S. Limber, "Why Should Parents and Educators Be Concerned About Cyber Bullying? International Bullying Prevention Association Conference, November 2007.

that frequently deals with purely written modes of communication and an inherent absence of nonverbal cues.

Second, individuals appalled at the degeneration of online civility need to speak out, to show that this type of behavior will no longer be tolerated. Targets of online hostility should also consider coming forward to show that attacks can have serious consequences. There are already several documented cases of teens taking their own lives because of cyberbullying.

Using the Internet Revolution Positively

A third step has to do with media literacy. People need to know how to differentiate between information that is published on legitimate sites that follow defined standards and also possibly a professional code of ethics, and information published in places like gossip sites whose only goal is to post the most outrageous headlines and stories in order to increase traffic. People can and will learn to shun and avoid such sites over time, particularly with education about why they are unethical.

Fourth, adult targets of online hostility deserve a national support network. This should be a safe place where they can congregate online to receive emotional support, practical advice on how to deal with transgressors, and information on whom to contact for legal advice when appropriate.

Finally, it's time to re-examine the current legal system. Online hostility is cross-jurisdictional. We might need laws that directly address this challenge. There is currently no uniformity of definition among states in the definition of cyberbullying and cyberharassment. Perhaps federal input is needed.

The Internet is bringing about a revolution in human knowledge and communication, and we have an unprecedented opportunity to make the global conversation more reasonable and productive. But we can only do so if we prevent the worst among us from silencing the best among us with hostility and incivility.

EVALUATING THE AUTHORS' ARGUMENTS:

Wales and Weckerle articulate five measures they think can help Americans be nicer to each other online. Identify these five measures and summarize each one. Then, state whether you agree that they can have a positive effect on online interactions. If so, why? If not, suggest another tactic or measure that you think might have a greater effect.

Electronically Monitoring Teens' Online Communications Can Prevent Cyberbullying

Elizabeth Charnock

"The best means for [detecting cyberbullying] is monitoring [kids'] electronic communications with each other."

In the following viewpoint Elizabeth Charnock argues that monitoring teens' online communications can prevent cyberbullying. She proposes that adults use automatic monitoring technology to troll students' online accounts and e-mails for patterns that could indicate whether cyberbullying is occurring. Charnock argues that the benefits from monitoring teens' online activity— keeping tabs on whom they communicate with, the nature of those communications, and whether a teen seems to be the target of cyberbullying—are worth violating a teen's privacy. Charnock concludes that only by monitoring teens' online communications can parents and school administrators stop cyberbullying at its source.

Elizabeth Charnock is the chief executive officer of Cataphora, a company that creates technologies addressing human behaviors related to electronic media, and the author of the book *The Digital You*.

AS YOU READ, CONSIDER THE FOLLOWING QUESTIONS:
1. Why is cyberbullying worse that traditional schoolyard bullying, according to Charnock?
2. What are the details of the automated monitoring system the author proposes to help curb cyberbullying?
3. Why does Charnock think merely filtering keywords is not sufficient to prevent cyberbullying?

As we live more of our lives online, a new phenomenon of hostile behavior has emerged on the Web that threatens to disrupt the way our kids live, learn and play. Cyberbullying is using the Internet, cell phones or other devices to send or post text or images intended to hurt or embarrass another person. For some, like 13-year-old Megan Meier, who in 2006 was the target of online taunting, cyberbullying can be fatal. Megan hanged herself after receiving a cruel MySpace message from her online boyfriend, "Josh"— a fictitious profile created by a classmate and her mother, Lori Drew.

Adults may assume that cyberbullying is less harmful to children and teens than its traditional, playground counterpart. But cases that result in suicide suggest that cyberbullying is just as—if not more—harmful than conventional schoolyard taunting.

What makes cyberbullying particularly distressing for its victims is the pervasive nature of the Internet and mobile phones. The "always-on" aspect of these technologies gives bullies easy access to victims, which means refuge is unavailable even in their own homes.

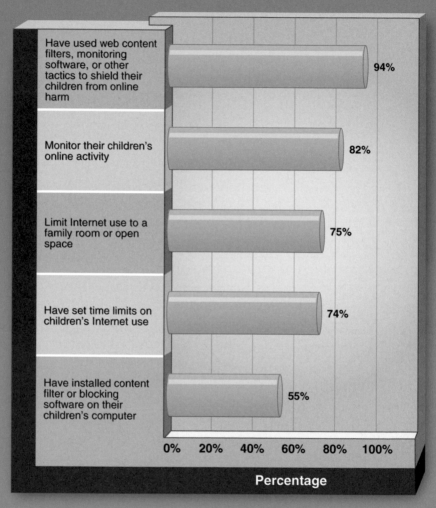

Parents Want to Monitor Their Children's Online Activity

The majority of parents support using monitoring and filtering software and other tactics to keep their children safe from online harm.

Have used web content filters, monitoring software, or other tactics to shield their children from online harm — 94%

Monitor their children's online activity — 82%

Limit Internet use to a family room or open space — 75%

Have set time limits on children's Internet use — 74%

Have installed content filter or blocking software on their children's computer — 55%

0% 20% 40% 60% 80% 100%

Percentage

Taken from: Harris Interactive Poll, August 10, 2006.

Parents Should Monitor Kids' Online Activity

Parents and educators can take several actions to protect our children. Foremost among them is increasing awareness. Parents need to know the inherent risks of the constantly evolving online environment. Early detection of cyberbullying is also critical to protecting kids. The best means for this is monitoring their electronic communications with each other and the adults in their lives. Despite concerns about invasion of student privacy, the benefits of monitoring electronic communications in school far outweigh potential risks. By adopting such policies, parents and school administrators gain the ability to uncover and rein in rumor-mongering, threats and harassment.

Technology Can Help

New technology that employs an integrated approach to analyzing online communication has the ability to uncover patterns that could flag cyberbullying. For example, teenagers often use strong language, and if an automated monitoring system issued an alert for every instance, system administrators would be overwhelmed with false alarms. When a student uses language that is negative, abusive or threatening, that may or may not indicate a problem. However, when the response is frightened or upset—or even the total silence of hiding in fear—this is a more reliable indicator of a problem. This approach is

Disney unveiled a cell phone with parental controls in 2006. More companies followed with parental-control devices.

far more effective than simply filtering for keywords, which fails to take into account the larger context of a child's online communication and what that shows about the child's interactions.

Because the problem of cyberbullying is, at heart, one centered around technology, it demands solutions equally as sophisticated and pervasive.

EVALUATING THE AUTHOR'S ARGUMENTS:

Charnock argues that monitoring teens' online communications is key to preventing cyberbullying from getting out of hand. Think about this proposal and how it might relate to your life. Have you ever been the victim of cyberbullying? If so, would it be worth it to have your MySpace, Facebook, or other online accounts monitored for your protection? Or, would you be unwilling to give up your privacy? Explain your reasoning and whether you support Charnock's ideas.

Electronically Monitoring Teens' Online Communications Can Destroy Trust

Esme Vos

"I fear that many parents will use technology—instead of taking time and making an effort—to try to figure out what's bothering their kids."

In the following viewpoint Esme Vos argues that parents should not use monitoring software to keep tabs on their children's online communications. Although monitoring software has helped some parents realize their children are having social problems, Vos thinks in general it is wrong to substitute technology for active parenting. In her opinion, children need to be talked to, not spied on. Discussing social problems with children is a better way to give them the tools they need to make healthy choices and confident decisions, both of which are likely to keep them out of trouble in a more meaningful and long-lasting way than simply spying on them can. For all of these reasons she urges parents not to monitor

Esme Vos, "Paralert: Safety Tool for Parents Monitoring Children's Online Activity," Pajama Entrepreneur.com, January 20, 2010. Reproduced by permission.

their teens' online communications but rather to build trust and cama-
raderie by talking to them about what is going on in their lives.

Esme Vos is the founder of Pajama Entrepreneur, a Web site about
online startup companies. She also runs the travel Web site Mapplr
and the fashion and style Web site Shopplr.

AS YOU READ, CONSIDER THE FOLLOWING QUESTIONS:

1. Describe in detail how the Paralert software works, as described
   by the author.
2. What, according to Vos, is a surefire way to break trust between
   a parent and a child?
3. How did reading her daughter's diary lead one mother to know
   less about her daughter, according to the author?

Paralert is an online tool for parents who want to spy on (oops,
monitor) their children's online activity. It is designed for parents of children between the ages of 6 [and] 15 years.

Paralert scans the child's activity in social networks and online chats,
and sends SMS [short message service] and email alerts to parents in real
time. Paralert uses a real time monitoring service that tracks the child's
activity on the computer on which it is installed. It detects the use of "suspicious" words and messages, and communicates data and screenshots to
the Paralert server. The server analyzes the data and automatically sends
alerts via email and SMS to the parents' mailbox or mobile phone. The
login-protected section of the website enables the parent to view information captured at the time of the alert, as well as additional information. This provides a context for the child's activity, enabling the parent
to assess the level of risk and offer appropriate assistance to the child.

Parents can define or remove "suspicious" words or phrases, according to the type of issue that they would like to monitor. They can also
modify the frequency of screenshots, and update profile information
such as email address and mobile phone number for alerts.

Origins of Paralert

Paralert was started in 2008 by Yehonatan (Yoni) Hasheli and Walla
Azrik in Israel. Yoni's experience in police intelligence and telco

[telecommunications] sales led to the concept of Paralert—to enable parents to monitor children's activity to help them identify risks such as sexual predators, cyberbullying and psychological disorders. Paralert has a distribution contract with one of Israel's leading ISPs [Internet service providers] (which has 33 percent of the Israel ISP market). Since then thousands of customers have joined the service through the ISP and via a direct online sales channel. The business is in the early stages, with the service commercially available in Israel (with thousands of customers). Paralert's founders are currently seeking angel funding to develop the second generation product and expand internationally.

Interview with Paralert

Where was Paralert founded? Why did you launch the service in Israel?

[Yoel Mittleberg, technology and business development representative for Paralert]: The business was founded in Israel. In addition, Israel has a very high level of usage of Internet amongst children, with a relatively small number of ISPs. This meant we could tap into a large portion of the market with few key relationships. We are now

Many parents think monitoring their kids' Internet usage is unnecessary.

planning to expand our operations, and offer the service to parents in other parts of the world, such as North America and Europe.

What are parents saying about the application? What do kids think? Don't the kids resent being spied on?

We have received extremely enthusiastic responses from parents, who have told us about life-threatening situations that have been identified using the software and handled before any harm came to the child. For example, one parent noticed that their child was researching websites of food disorders and it was then that they realized she was anorexic. Another parent identified an urgent suicide risk and was able to intervene before anything happened.

On the one hand, parents would probably prefer not to spy on the kids, but on the other hand, realizing that these risks are out there and very real, they are determined to use any tool they can to protect their children.

The software can be run in overt or covert mode. Some children are told about its presence, as part of their disciplinary framework at home. It is quite common, even for parents who do not use parental controls, to regularly read their child's emails or chat transcripts. When this is done as part of an educational relationship, children apparently accept it, understand the need and cooperate. Other children would not be aware that the software is installed, until an emergency happens and the parent intervenes. In that scenario, there are often more pressing issues at stake, such as the danger from meeting a stranger, or potential life-threatening situations.

Parents Should Not Spy on Kids

I believe that there are a lot of parents who are terrified about the dangers of the Internet. They justify spying on their children's online activity as a "normal" way to be a parent. If the children know this is happening and assent to it, it's not spying. However, if the children don't and if they later find out that the parent has been spying, the trust is broken. Once broken it is very difficult to repair. What happens then is that the child will hide things from the parent, not just on-line activity. The child will be reluctant to talk to the parent about friendships, feelings, school performance, sex, and other issues that are bothering him or her.

This is a very dangerous game for a parent to play. I remember an incident that happened to a close school friend when I was in my teens. My school friend discovered that her mother had been reading her diary (which my friend had taken great care to hide in her closet). It was such a great shock and disappointment to her. My friend's trust in her mother was completely destroyed. She stopped talking to her mother about the things that bothered her. Result: the mother ended up knowing much less about her daughter than if she had *not* secretly read the diary.

No Substitute for Good Parenting

It's much easier to use technology to spy on children rather than tak-ing the time to build a sincere and long-lasting relationship of trust. I fear that many parents will use technology—instead of taking time and making an effort—to try to figure out what's bothering their kids.

EVALUATING THE AUTHORS' ARGUMENTS:

In this viewpoint Vos argues that good parenting, rather than technology, can solve teen social problems like cy-berbullying. In the previous viewpoint, Elizabeth Charnock argued that since cyberbullying is a technological prob-lem, technology should be part of the solution. After read-ing both viewpoints, what do you think? What role, if any, should technology play in preventing cyberbullying? Quote from the viewpoints you have read in your answer.

Facts About Cyberbullying

According to I-SAFE, a nonprofit organization dedicated to Internet safety:
- 42 percent of kids have been cyberbullied.
- One in four have had it happen more than once.
- 35 percent of kids have been threatened while online.
- Almost one in five have had it happen more than once.
- 21 percent of kids have received mean or threatening e-mails or other messages.
- 58 percent of kids say someone has said mean or hurtful things to them online.
- More than four out of ten say it has happened more than once.
- 53 percent of kids admit to having said something mean or hurtful to or about another person online.
- More than one in three have done it more than once.
- 58 percent have not told their parents or another adult about something mean or hurtful that happened to them online.

A February 2010 survey by the Cyberbullying Research Center found the following about teens and cyberbullying:
- 20.7 percent of teens said they had been cyberbullied at least once in their lifetime.
- 15.9 percent of boys and 25.8 percent of girls reported having been cyberbullied at some point in their life.
- 7.1 percent of boys said they had been cyberbullied in the last thirty days.
- 7.9 percent of girls said they had been cyberbullied in the last thirty days.
- 17 percent of teens reported they had been cyberbullied two or more times in the last thirty days.
- 13.7 percent said they had received mean or hurtful comments in the last thirty days.
- 12.9 percent said they had had rumors spread about them online in the last thirty days.

- Girls are significantly more likely to have experienced cyberbullying in their lifetimes: 25.8 percent of girls said they had been cyberbullied, versus 16 percent of boys.
- Girls are more likely to cyberbully others; girls are 21.1 percent likely to have cyberbullied someone, versus 18.3 percent of boys.
- Girls are more likely to spread rumors, while boys are more likely to post hurtful pictures or videos.

According to the National Crime Prevention Center:

- More than 40 percent of all teenagers with Internet access have reported being bullied online.
- Girls are more likely than boys to be the target of cyberbullying.
- Just 10 percent of kids who have been cyberbullied told their parents about the incident.
- Just 18 percent of cyberbullying cases are reported to a local or national law enforcement agency.
- Sixty percent of those who have been bullied said they had not told their parents about the incident.
- The most common virtual locations for cyberbullying are chat rooms, social networking Web sites, e-mail, and instant messaging systems.
- Fifty-eight percent of fourth through eighth graders reported having had mean or cruel things said to them online.
- Fifty-three percent admitted that they had said mean or hurtful things to others while online.
- Ten percent of teens reported they had been made to feel "threatened, embarrassed or uncomfortable" by a photo taken of them using a cell phone camera.

According to a survey conducted by the National Campaign:

- Overall, 20 percent of teenagers had sent or posted nude or semi-nude pictures or video of themselves.
- 22 percent of girls had sent such pictures or video.
- 18 percent of boys had sent such pictures or video.
- 39 percent of all teenagers had sent or posted sexually suggestive messages.
- 37 percent of girls had sent or posted such messages.
- 40 percent of boys had sent or posted such messages.
- 71 percent of teen girls and 67 percent of teen boys who had sent or posted sexually suggestive content said they had sent or posted this content to a boyfriend or girlfriend.

Organizations to Contact

American Psychological Association (APA)
750 First St. NE
Washington, DC 20002-4242
(800) 374-2721
e-mail: public.affairs@apa.org
Web site: www.apa.org

The APA is the primary scientific and professional psychology organization in the United States. Its official position is that all forms of bullying exert short- and long-term harmful psychological effects on both bullies and their victims. Available resources include the *APA Resolution on Bullying Among Children and Youth* (supporting H.R. 1589, the Bullying and Gang Reduction for Improved Education Act of 2009). The APA Web site offers links to a research roundup, bullying prevention programs around the world, and a Getting Help section for adolescents dealing with bullying issues.

American School Counselor Association (ASCA)
1101 King St., Suite 625
Alexandria, VA 22314
(703) 683-2722; toll-free: (800) 306-4722
fax: (703) 683-1619
Web site: www. schoolcounselor.org

ASCA sponsors workshops such as "Bullying and What to Do About It" and publishes the bimonthly magazine *ASCA School Counselor.* Free online resources include the articles "The Buzz on Bullying" and "Appropriate Use of the Internet." The association's online bookstore offers titles aimed at young people such as *Cool, Calm, and Confident: A Workbook to Help Kids Learn Assertiveness Skills;* antibullying posters, banners, and bulletin boards; and sample lesson plans for school-based anti-bullying programs.

Center for Safe and Responsible Internet Use

474 W. Twenty-Ninth Ave.
Eugene, OR 97405
(541) 556-1145
e-mail: nwillard@csriu.org
Web site: www.cyberbully.org

The center was founded in 2002 by Nancy Willard, an authority on student Internet use management in schools and the author of *Cyberbullying and Cyberthreats: Responding to the Challenge of Online Social Aggression, Threats, and Distress.* In addition to briefs and guides for educators and parents, the center offers numerous reports, articles, and books for student researchers, including "Sexting and Youth: Achieving a Rational Approach," "Why Age and Identity Verification Will Not Work," and *Cyber-Safe Kids, Cyber-Savvy Teens.*

Centers for Disease Control and Prevention (CDC)

National Center for Injury Prevention and Control
4770 Buford Hwy. NE, MS F-63
Atlanta, GA 30341-3717
toll-free: (800) 232-4636
e-mail: cdcinfo@cdc.gov
Web site: www. cdc.gov/ViolencePrevention/youthviolence/schoolviolence/

The CDC is the federal agency responsible for monitoring and responding to public health threats in the United States. It lists physical bullying and social rejection as individual risk factors for youth violence, including school shootings and suicide. It conducts research on the causes, consequences, and prevention of cyberbullying and offers numerous reports and guides on the subject through its Web site.

CyberMentors (Beatbullying)

Units 1 + 4
Belvedere Road
London SE19 2AT
United Kingdom
44+ 208 771 3377
e-mail: admin@beatbullying.org
Web site: http://cybermentors.org.uk

This organization, run by leading UK bullying prevention charity Beatbullying, is an online social networking service that offers advice to those affected by cyberbullying. Victims of cyberbullying use the site to contact other teens who have been trained to offer advice and support. Beatbullying counselors are on call to take appropriate action to protect individuals from further attacks.

Gay, Lesbian, and Straight Education Network (GLSEN)

90 Broad St., 2nd Fl.
New York, NY 10004
(212) 727-0135
fax: (212) 727-0254
e-mail: glsen@glsen.org
Web site: www.glsen.org

Founded in 1990, GLSEN fosters a healthy, safe school environment where every student is respected regardless of sexual orientation. It is the oversight organization of more than four thousand school-based Gay-Straight Alliances (GSAs) and the sponsor of two antidiscrimination school events, the National Day of Silence and No Name-Calling Week. Its anti-bullying initiatives include the educational Web site ThinkB4YouSpeak.com and the monthly e-newsletter *Respect Report*. The GLSEN Web site offers research reports such as *From Teasing to Torment: School Climate in America; A National Report on School Bullying* and *Shared Differences: The Experiences of Lesbian, Gay, Bisexual, and Transgender Students of Color* and an anti-bullying toolkit called the New Safe Space Kit.

Make a Difference for Kids

People's Bank of Mt. Washington
PO Box 95
Mt. Washington, KY 40047
toll-free hotline: 800-273-TALK (8255)
e-mail: donna@makeadifferenceforkids.org
Web site: www.makeadifferenceforkids.org

This organization promotes awareness and prevention of cyberbullying and suicide through education. It was created in memory of

Rachael Neblett and Kristin Settles, two Kentucky teens who committed suicide as a result of being cyberbullied. The organization runs a cyberbullying hotline and encourages kids in crisis to call them.

National Center for Bullying Prevention
PACER Center
8161 Normandale Blvd.
Bloomington, MN 55437
toll-free: (888) 248-0822
fax: (952) 838-0199
Web site: www.pacer.org/bullying

Funded by U.S. Department of Education's Office of Special Education Programs, the center is an advocate for children with disabilities and all children subjected to bullying, from elementary through high school. Bullying and cyberbullying prevention resources (available in English, Spanish, Hmong, and Somali) include audio-video clips, reading lists, creative writing exercises, group activities, and numerous downloadable handouts such as "Bullying Fast Facts." The center sponsors school and community workshops and events such as National Bullying Awareness Week each October.

National Crime Prevention Council (NCPC)
2345 Crystal Dr., Suite 500
Arlington, VA 22202
(202) 466-6272
fax: (202) 296-1356
Web site: www.ncpc.org/topics/cyberbullying

The council, a partnership of the U.S. Department of Justice and private sponsors such as the Wireless Foundation and the Ad Council, was founded in 1979 to get citizens, especially youth, involved in crime prevention. It is best known for televised public service announcements and school-based programs featuring McGruff the Crime Dog. Other novel approaches to addressing social problems include the Community Responses to Drug Abuse and Youth Outreach for Victim Assistance programs. The council's cyberbullying campaign includes a public service ad contest (winning ads are viewable on the Web site), free anti-bullying banners users can copy and paste into e-mail or social networking pages, the Be Safe and Sound in School program, and educational training manuals for youth and adults to manage bullying and intimidation. Downloadable resources include a range of podcasts and research papers, including the Harris Interactive report/poll *Teens and Cyberbullying.*

Olweus Bullying Prevention Program
Institute on Family & Neighborhood Life
Clemson University
158 Poole Agricultural Center
Clemson, SC 29634-0132
toll-free: (864) 710-4562
fax: (406)-862-8971
e-mail: nobully@clemson.edu
Web site: www.clemson.edu/olweus

The program, developed by Norwegian bullying researcher Dan Olweus (ol-VAY-us) in the 1980s, is a school-based intervention program designed to prevent or reduce bullying in elementary, middle, and junior high schools (students six to fifteen years old). It is endorsed as a model anti-bullying program by the U.S. government's Substance Abuse and Mental Health Services Administration and the Office of Juvenile Justice and Delinquency Prevention. How the program works, statistical outcomes, and studies of the effectiveness of this and other anti-bullying programs are available on its Web site.

Wired Safety
1 Bridge St.
Irvington-on-Hudson, NY 10533
(201) 463-8663
fax: (201) 670-7002
e-mail: parry@aftab.com
Web sites: www.wiredsafety.org; www.stopcyberbullying.org

Under executive director Parry Aftab, Wired Safety is an Internet safety and help group that offers articles, activities, and advice designed for seven- to seventeen-year-olds on a range of issues including cyberbullying, cyberstalking, and harassment. Resources include a Cyber 911 Help Line, a cyberstalking poll, cyberbullying Q&As, and a speakers bureau. Information available on the Web sites covers Facebook privacy protection, how to handle sexting, building safe Web sites, and many other topics. Wired Safety also sponsors the annual WiredKids Summit on Capitol Hill; in a role reversal, tech-savvy teens get the chance there to present cyber safety research, raise cyberbullying issues, and tell industry and government leaders what they need to know about cyber safety.

For Further Reading

Books

Hinduja, Sameer, and Justin W. Patchin. *Bullying Beyond the Schoolyard: Preventing and Responding to Cyberbullying*. Thousand Oaks, CA: Sage, 2008.

Jacobs, Thomas A. *Teen Cyberbullying Investigated: Where Do Your Rights End and Consequences Begin?* Minneapolis: Free Spirit, 2010.

Kowalski, Robin M., Susan P. Limber, and Patricia W. Agatston. *Cyber Bullying: Bullying in the Digital Age*. Hoboken, NJ: Wiley-Blackwell, 2008.

McQuade III, Samuel C., James P. Colt, and Nancy B.B. Meyer. *Cyber Bullying: Protecting Kids and Adults from Online Bullies*. Westport, CT: Praeger, 2009.

Rogers, Vanessa. *Cyberbullying: Activities to Help Children and Teens to Stay Safe in a Texting, Twittering, Social Networking World*. London: Jessica Kingsley, 2010.

Willard, Nancy E. *Cyberbullying and Cyberthreats: Responding to the Challenge of Online Social Aggression, Threats, and Distress*. Champaign, IL: Research Press, 2007.

Periodicals and Internet Sources

ADL on the Frontline. "Saying No to Online Hate," Summer 2009.

Anti-Defamation League. *Bullying/Cyberbullying Prevention Law*, April 2009. www.adl.org/civil_rights/Anti-Bullying%20Law%20Toolkit_2009.pdf.

Celizic, Mike. "Her Teen Committed Suicide over 'Sexting': Cynthia Logan's Daughter Was Taunted About Photo She Sent to Boyfriend," MSNBC, March 6, 2009. http://today.msnbc.msn.com/id/29546030/.

Collins, Lauren. "Friend Game: Behind the Online Hoax That Led to a Girl's Suicide," *New Yorker*, January 21, 2008. www.newyorker.com/reporting/2008/01/21/080121fa_fact_collins.

Dowd, Maureen. "Stung by the Perfect Sting," *New York Times*, August 26, 2009. www.nytimes.com/2009/08/26/opinion/26dowd.html.

Feinberg, Ted, and Nicole Robey. "Cyberbullying," *Principal Leadership*, September 2008. www.nasponline.org/resources/principals/Cyberbulling%20NASSP%209-08.pdf.

Foxman, Abraham H., and Cyndi Silverman. "Cyberbullying: A Growing Menace," Anti-Defamation League, 2009. www.adl.org/ADL_Opinions/Anti_Semitism_Domestic/Cyberbullying_A_Growing_Menace.htm.

Jones, Jessica. "Cyberbullying Is Not OK—It Is a Crime," *Daily Telegraph* (London), August 16, 2007. www.dailytelegraph.com.au/news/classmate/cyber-bullying-is-a-crime/story-e6frewti-1111114190823.

Kowalski, Robin M., and Susan P. Limber. "Electronic Bullying Among Middle School Students," *Journal of Adolescent Health,* vol. 41, 2007. www.jahonline.org/article/S1054-139X(07)00361-8/fulltext.

Leichtling, Ben. "Effective Laws Can Stop Cyberbullying, Harassment and Abuse," Bullies Be Gone, October 27, 2009. www.bulliesbegoneblog.com/2009/10/27/effective-laws-can-stop-cyber-bullying-harassment-and-abuse/.

Lenhart, Amanda. "Teens and Sexting," Pew Internet and American Life Project, December 15, 2009. www.pewinternet.org/~/media//Files/Reports/2009/PIP_Teens_and_Sexting.pdf.

Levine, Judith. "What's the Matter with Teen Sexting?" *American Prospect*, February 2, 2009. www.prospect.org/cs/articles?article=whats_the_matter_with_teen_sexting.

Los Angeles Times. "Overreaction to Online Harassment," August 22, 2009. http://articles.latimes.com/2009/aug/22/opinion/ed-cyberbullying22.

Marshall, Penny. "Generation Sexting: What Teenage Girls Really Get Up to on the Internet Should Chill Every Parent," *Daily Mail* (London), March 18, 2009. www.dailymail.co.uk/femail/article-1162777/Generation-sexting-What-teenage-girls-really-internet-chill-parent.html.

Meech, Scott. "Cyber Bullying: Worse than Traditional Bullying," TechLearning, May 1, 2007. www.techlearning.com/article/7284.

New York Times. "Vague Cyberbullying Law," September 8, 2009. www.nytimes.com/2009/09/08/opinion/08tue2.html.

Patchin, Justin W., and Sameer Hinduja. "Cyberbullying: An Exploratory Analysis of Factors Related to Offending and Victimization," *Deviant Behavior*, March/April, 2008.

Rede, George. "'Sexting' Solution: Teach Teens Self-Respect," *Portland Oregonian*, April 4, 2009. www.oregonlive.com/opinion/index .ssf/2009/04/sexting_solutions_teach_teens.html.

Rommelmann, Nancy. "Anatomy of a Child Pornographer," *Reason*, July 2009. http://reason.com/archives/2009/06/04/anatomy-of-a-child-pornographe/2.

Seattle Times. "Zero Tolerance for Cyber Bullies," January 21, 2010. http://seattletimes.nwsource.com/html/editorials/2010857333_edit 22mcclure.html.

Sheehan, Paul. "I Married an Ascham Bully," *Sydney Morning Herald* (Australia), May 11, 2009. www.smh.com.au/opinion/i-married-an-ascham-bully-20090510-az41.html?page=-1.

Solove, Daniel. "More Misguided Responses to the Megan Meier Incident," Concurring Opinions, May 18, 2008. www.concurring opinions.com/archives/2008/05/more_misguided.html.

Szoka Berin, and Adam Thierer. "Cyberbullying Legislation: Why Education Is Preferable to Regulation," *Progress on Point*, June 2009. http://pff.org/issues-pubs/pops/2009/pop16.12-cyberbullying-ed ucation-better-than-regulation.pdf.

Torrence, Samantha A. "The Anonymous Advantage," *Digital Journal*, December 8, 2007. www.digitaljournal.com/article/247159/ Op_Ed_The_Anonymous_Advantage.

Volokh, Eugene. "Federal Felony to Use Blogs, the Web, etc. to Cause Substantial Emotional Distress Through 'Severe, Repeated, and Hostile' Speech?" Volokh Conspiracy, April 30, 2009. http://volokh .com/posts/1241122059.shtml.

———. "Rep. Linda Sanchez Defends Proposed Outlawing of Using Blogs, the Web, etc. to Cause Substantial Emotional Distress Through 'Severe, Repeated, and Hostile Speech,'" Volokh Conspiracy, May 7, 2009. http://volokh.com/archives/archive_2009_05_03-2009_05_09.shtml#1241740320.

Walsh, David. "Ending the National Panic on Sexting," *Los Angeles Times*, June 22, 2009. www.latimes.com/news/opinion/opinionla/la-oew-walsh22-2009jun22,0,4020842.story.

Web Sites

Cyberbullying.ca (www.cyberbullying.ca). This Canadian site offers useful facts about cyberbullying, along with helpful prevention strategies. It is run by Bill Belsey, the creator of www.bullying.org.

Cyberbullying Prevention (www.cyberbullyingprevention.com). This site offers prevention tips, workshops, and educational videos for those seeking to put an end to cyberbullying.

Cyberbullying Resource Center (www.cyberbullying.us). This site is dedicated to providing up-to-date information about the nature, extent, causes, and consequences of cyberbullying among adolescents. It serves as a clearinghouse of information concerning the ways adolescents use and misuse technology. It is intended to be a resource for parents, educators, law enforcement officers, counselors, and others who work with youth and is a good place to find facts, figures, and detailed stories from those who have been directly impacted by online aggression. In addition, the site includes numerous resources to help prevent and respond to cyberbullying incidents.

Wired Safety (www.wiredsafety.org). Wired Safety is the world's largest Internet safety, help, and education resource. The Web site offers valuable information for parents, educators, and students about how to prevent cyberbullying. In addition to information on cyberbullying, information about social networking and cyber dating is also available.

Index

telling a friend, 74
of victims on reaction to being
cyberbullied, 14, *85*
of victims on types/locations
of victimizations, *15*

T
Teenagers
monitoring e-communications
of, 93–97
with profiles on social
networking sites, 86
suicides and, 35
Turley, Jonathan, 64, *68*

U
University of
California–Berkeley, 96

V
Victims
effects of being cyberbullied
on, *78*
legal protection and, 72–73
reactions to cyberbullying

among, *85*
reasons for not reporting
cyberbullying, 14, 16
types/locations of
cyberbullying, *15*
Vos, Esme, 93

W
Wales, Jimmy, 82
Wall Street Journal (newspaper),
53
Weckerle, Andrea, 82
Willard, Nancy, 12
WiredSafety.org (Web site), 13,
41
Wolfe, Billy, 67
World Health Organization
(WHO), 35

Y
Yale University School of
Medicine, 14

Z
Zero tolerance policies, 79

Picture Credits

© Ace Stock Limited/Alamy, 34
Mario Anzuoni/Reuters/Landov, 60
AP Images, 38, 48
Cengage/Gale, 15, 21, 27, 56, 66, 78, 85, 90
© David Crausby/Alamy, 63, 72
© Leila Cutler/Alamy, 95
Sarah Dussault/MCT/Landov, 80
Spencer Grant/Photo Researchers, Inc., 13
Bill Greenblatt/UPI/Landov, 42
Bryan Haraway/Getty Images, 91
Nicholas Kamm/AFP/Getty Images, 20
© By Ian Miles–Flashpoint Pictures/Alamy, 28
© Mark Philips/Alamy, 10
Picture Partners/Photo Researchers, Inc., 84
Chip Somodevilla/Getty Images, 68
Roger L. Wollenberg/UPI/Landov, 54